LENT PRAYERS AND MEDITATIONS

A day-by-day-devotional guide.

LENT PRAYERS AND MEDITATIONS

A day-by-day-devotional guide.

by
Aida M. Rabenhorst

E-BookTime, LLC
Montgomery, Alabama

Lent Prayers and Meditations
A day-by-day-devotional guide.

First Edition
Published February 2016
E-BookTime, LLC
6598 Pumpkin Road
Montgomery, AL 36108
www.e-booktime.com

Library of Congress Control Number: 2016933620

ISBN: 978-1-60862-636-6

Printed in United States of America

To order a copy of this book and other books written by the author, please go to e-booktime.com, Amazon.com, BarnesandNoble.com or BooksaMillion.com

This book is dedicated to my loving family.

Table of Contents

Our Father Who art in heaven, in the name of Your Son Jesus Christ, may You grace this book I pray to serve the purpose of spreading Your Word regarding Your Son's life of passion through prayers and meditations contained herein. May every Christian and non-Christian, or of any type of denomination who might happen to read this book be blest with patience, understanding and time to absorb what little information were written in this book regarding the events that happened in the life of Your Son when He once graced us to come down here on earth from Your heaven's kingdom. I pray that the prayers, meditations, and Bible verses quoted herein will be pondered upon, their meanings received in the graciousness with which they are sent to the reader.

Opening Prayer

Loving Lord, as I enter this Lent period to observe this time of holy days, help me to set aside my whole self to remember You and to journey with You during Your life of passion here on earth. Before You my Lord, I set to give my heart, mind and soul to follow You.

I pray O Lord to bless my soul, work within me that I may learn to deny myself from things of this world. Help me to forget myself that I may willingly take up my own cross without a moan. Lead me to a life depending only on You that I may bear much fruit so that I may live a richer life with You.

I pray with ardent love doing penance, abstaining, fasting and confessing with sentiments to You O Lord of love that I may follow Your footsteps in order for me to be worthy of Your promises, for "all Christians believe that one day we will all be raised in a glorious form and then be caught up and rendered immaculate to be with You forever"[1]. May Your blessings Lord Jesus, the love of God the Father, and the communion of the Holy Spirit be with us all. Amen.

---

1 1 Thessalonians 4:17; Revelation 21:27

The 1st Four Days of Lent

Day 1, Ash Wednesday – Turn Away from Sin

"By the sweat of your brow you will eat your food until you return to the ground, since from it you were taken; for dust you are and to dust you will return."[2]

Almighty and Eternal God, as I begin my Lenten Season in the lowliness of my heart, help me to remember that I come from dust and to dust I shall return. In my failure to listen to Your Holy Spirit's guidance, I sorrowfully repent for all my sins. Help me Father to turn away from sin that I may return back to You with all my heart and soul.

Beloved Lord Jesus, You rose from death through shame and suffering because of my sins. I sunk in shame, grieving and lamenting by the way You met Your end here with us on earth. Forgive me Lord, my Savior, for all the sufferings You endured because of me, and of my sins of which I bitterly regret.

I thank You Lord God for Your unending love, Your life, teachings, examples, miracles, sufferings and death – Your way for us to see Your encompassing love and passion. Now You dwell in heaven and sits at the right Hand of the Father. May all hearts be changed to turn to You, for all lives here on earth to be turned around, not in shame, grief or sorrow but refreshed with Your unending love.

Daily thoughts of God through prayers and meditations make our heart merge with the heart of Jesus.

---

2 Genesis 3:19

Meditation

The beauty of this world You have given us
is beyond description;
Like You, it's beauty is eternal,
like You, it is without sin.
The sweet joys we get from its magnificence
is far too great for us sinful humans
who will someday perish
from this magnificent creation of Yours.

Lord God, I need Your guidance
for my soul to be freed from sinfulness
as my heart desires to live in
blessed days of righteousness.
Light my path and let me be a part
of Your eternal world
that I may not turn to dust and ashes
but be one with You,
Your Son and the Holy Spirit
forever and ever. Amen.

The 1st Four Days of Lent

Day 2, Thursday – Ask for Forgiveness

"The Lord regretted that he had made human beings on the earth, and his heart was deeply troubled."[3]

Holy God, as I enter into the spirit of this painful season of Lent, I beg You for the forgiveness of our wickedness that caused Your loving heart to grieve. Great was our sin that caused You tears and sorrow, and great was Your Son's love that He with the concurrence of the Holy Spirit offered Himself for the atonement of our sins. Have mercy on us inspite of us being sinners as we are. We sin against our mind, against our own soul, against our own body, but mostly against You my God, please forgive us.

Lord Jesus, as You stand outside the closed doors of our souls to be let in, help us to have ears to hear You knocking, grant our lips to answer: 'Yes O Lord, Your servant is here.' Blessed Lord, grant our eyes to see Your brightness as You reveal Your ever shining light upon us. Grant our hearts to yearn for Your presence. Help us to fight against all evil, teach us to strive for obedience to be conformed to the likeness of You, and so to rejoice in Your righteousness to be made fit for the everlasting joy of heaven, all this I ask in Your holy and blessed name's sake. Amen.

His thirst is extreme, we could never know it's depth for what do we know? If we only knew how intense it is, we would do our hardest to quench it; we could start by opening the door of our hearts.

---

3 Genesis 6:6

Meditation

What You did for love is beyond measure,
great is Your mercy.
Unending mercy for unrepenting souls
who fear not of torment and punishment,
let alone God Himself.

Lord, forgive us, rescue us from threats
and dangers of our own sins.
With Your power, "Let us lay aside the
works of darkness, and put on
the armor of Light.

Let us walk becomingly as in the day,
not in revelry and drunkenness,
not in debauchery and wantonness,
not in strife and jealousy.
But put on the Lord Jesus Christ."[4]

---

4 Romans 13:12-14

The 1ˢᵗ Four Days of Lent

Day 3, Friday – Call Upon God for Guidance

"I love the Lord, because He has heard my voice and my supplications. Because He has inclined His ear to me, Therefore I will call upon Him as long as I live."[5]

O Mighty and Eternal Father, with my head bowed down to You, I, who am not worthy to speak to You, look at You or be in Your presence, hereby humbly invoke Your blessed name for I believe in You, I hope in You and I trust in Your truth forever. I pray for Your guidance.

Beloved Jesus, how wonderful it is to have a friend like You. Blessed are You who hear our prayers in the day and our cries in the night. You lovingly come to our aid whenever we need You. Lord, lead our hearts and souls to the fullness of Your mystery and truth; sanctify our hearts, cleanse our souls, and purify our bodies that evil may not dwell within us.

O Glorious Holy Spirit of God, Guest of my soul, I call upon You, Spirit of the world whose endless light never fails. Guide my mind, illumine my soul, and fill my heart with Your love, that I may sin no more. In the name of our beloved Lord Jesus Christ who lives and reigns with God the Father and the Holy Spirit forever and ever. Amen.

God promised that He will never leave us,
may we never forsake Him.

---

5 Psalm 28

Meditation

O Prince of Peace
Protector of my soul and body,
bless me with Your Holy Spirit
to guide me for my soul aches
to be good, just and holy.

Let me not wander away from You
O Lord, as my body gets carried by
this life's torrent stream.
Bless me and enable me
to follow You.

Come, take possession of my heart
make it clean and pure for I am eager
to come to You whom I follow,
trust, believe in, and love
most ardently!

The 1st Four Days of Lent

Day 4, Saturday – Prayer to be Humble

*"He has told you, O man, what is good; And what does the
LORD require of you But to do justice, to love kindness,
And to walk humbly with your God?"*[6]

Jesus, fount of mercy, You came in perfect humility giving
up Your life in complete obedience, help me to recognize
the lowest point of Your life here on earth during the hours
of Your suffering. Increase in me the acknowledgement of
my sinfulness that I, as a human being may have a way to be
humble. May my love for others increase and overflow, and
my love for myself decrease and cease.

May You bless me with a gentle and lowly heart for me to
humble myself before You for I know that You detest the
proud of heart. May I be willing to learn from Your
examples in order to attain a clear understanding of Your
teachings as I hope for an eternal life with You, which You
promised in Your glorious gospel, O Beloved Lord Jesus
Christ to whose name I kneel and pray. Amen.

*If the sound of God is not clear and the heart doesn't feel, perhaps all
we need to do is to stop and be still.*

---

6 Micah 6:8

Meditation

Blessed are those unique few
whose hearts are meek
where You O Lord find rest
as in the heart of Your gentle monk
whom You've blest exceedingly
to receive what others consider
misfortune and dishonor.
Oh how blessed was his heart,
one resigned to suffer
for his Lord Jesus.

Lord, bless my heart to
receive the same fortune and benefit
from the lowliness of heart
as Venerable Cyrus showed to his persecutors.
Bless me to deny myself
for nothing is more acceptable to You
than for a soul to give no thought to pleasure.
Guide my footsteps toward You
whose name be all the glory
and praise forever and ever.

The 1st Week of Lent

Day 5, First Sunday – Examination of Conscience

"Stand in awe, and sin not: commune with your own heart upon your bed, and be still. Selah"[7]

"Search me, O God, and know my heart; Try me and know my anxious thoughts."[8] You know my thoughts and my offenses. Lord grace me to restrain my senses to be free from earthly distractions. Let me seek to be in solitude in the privacy of my room that I may commune with my own heart where You are, still and unseen. As I lay still on my bed, help me to earnestly examine my conscience so as to be enlightened to see only the log that is in my own eye. Blind me to the offenses I receive from others for I should be grateful for any misdeeds done to me, and to accept them in complete humility.

In my quiet room Father, may You communicate Your will to my soul for me to lead a spiritual life protected by Your grace. Grant my soul not to be afraid but be content in order for me to progress with joy as I separate myself from all the burdens created by my con-science. Grant me peace when trouble ensue me that I may have a sweet rest, as Solomon said: "When you lie down, you will not be afraid; when you lie down, your sleep will be sweet."[9]

Life's tragedies are trials to help transform us and make us closer to God.

7 Psalm 4:4
8 Psalm 139:23
9 Proverb 3:24

Meditation

Dear God,
how appalling have we become to You,
we who do not take heed to Your decrees,
and so lightly do we take Your warnings
that we've lost sight of Your commandments,
forgive us Father for what we've become.

As I examine my conscience
I can't help but reminisce of the olden days
when parents didn't shy of reminding their young
to have fear of the Lord as we gazed upon the sky.
'Trust in the Lord, Thy God' they said as we stood
by the Image of Your Sacred heart.

They fed young minds with Your love,
they nourished our souls with Your peace
and filled our conscience with moral sense.
Now the busyness of life occupies our minds
rather than concern for eternal life.
O merciful Father, help us all to be fixed on You,
and not on this world.

The 1st Week of Lent

Day 6, Monday – Prayer Before Communion

"I am the living bread that came down from heaven.
Whoever eats this bread will live forever. This bread is my
flesh, which I will give for the life of the world."[10]

Eternal Father, let not the above verse be taken for granted by anyone. Bless all hearts and souls to surrender to You that we may be blessed even further to come to Your sacred temple to receive You through Communion. Lord, thank You for allowing this grain of sand to renounce its entire self to Your loving hand. In Your presence, I humbly offer You my tender love and affection in reparation for all of my sins confessing my grief and sorrow over my faults and weaknesses that I have yet to overcome.

Lord, as I approach You at Your altar, I thank You for the precious Life, Body and Blood You gave up. I cry out loud to You, here I am consecrating my whole insignificant essence with all its ardent affection. I pray for my love for You to increase a thousandfold that I may taste Your sweet love and may it be preserved in me to produce Your sweetness on to others. I pray for the purity of my heart that it may be immersed in Your holy Blood. In Your mercy O God, remember me in Your grace, bless me to love You more than anything else in this whole universe for I want to live with You forever. Amen.

God promised His eternal love. Indeed He is worthy of all
honor, praise, and above all, our eternal love.

---

10 John 6:51

Meditation

O Lord Jesus Christ,
I, unworthy of all, humbly beg You
to stay close by my side, sit beside me
as I bow my head in repentance.
Yearning with all its affection
I open wide my heart to You.
The soul of my lips thirsts
as I eagerly await to approach You,
to taste Your holy Body and Blood
that I may be wholly united to You.

By the mystery and grace
of Your holy sacrament
my hunger and thirst would be satisfied
for You alone are my meat and drink,
O what joy deep inside my heart You bring.
I shall never hunger for I remember You say:
"I am the living bread which came down
from heaven: if any man eat of this bread,
he shall live for ever: and the bread that I will give
is my flesh, which I will give
for the life of the world.[11]

---

11 John 6:51

The 1st Week of Lent

Day 7, Tuesday – Thanksgiving for the Holy Communion

"While they were eating, Jesus took bread, and when he had given thanks, he broke it and gave it to his disciples, saying, "Take and eat; this is my body.""[12]

Creator of the universe and Overseer of all life, this smallest grain of Your creation who is not worthy to give You thanks for all the glory You have created for who could be worthy enough to stand and give You thanks for all the blessings of love You have showered upon us? Only Your Son Jesus Christ, the Lamb is worthy of all the glory. There are no words to thank You Lord God for the way You reached out to our undeserving souls in order to save us from our sins with Your precious Life and holy Blood.

Unworthy of all, I thank You Lord for coming into my life. I thank You for opening the eye of my mind, heart and soul to You. I thank You for granting me the privilege to partake in the holy communion wherewith You quench my hunger for a taste of Your sweet body, and quench my thirst for a sift of Your holy Blood. Thank You so ever for allowing my soiled feet to step into Your holy church and letting my dirty fingers to touch You every time I come to receive You. And how very grateful my soul is for allowing it to reach this height of joy every time I come in communion with You.

12 Matthew 26:26

Grant O Lord for everyone to open their hearts to You, bless their hands to reach out to You, their knees to bend down before You, and their heads to bow down to You for all eyes to see the beauty of Your love. May all hearts love You O blessed Jesus, in Your most holy name I pray. Amen.

Jesus rejoices when we receive Him in the Eucharist.
Let us thank Him for coming down each time
where we share in His divinity.

Meditation

What a bliss it is
to receive the fruit of Your Blood
for You refresh my thirsty soul.
O divine, You touch my heart
and give me hope to make eternity mine.
How do I thank a Lord
whom I love more than life?

Down on my knees I come to You
to thank You Lord God of heaven
for without Your gentle love
there is no living, life's undone.
You nourish my world without end
for upon the table where You sat
You gave me bread and drink.

Though I'm stained with sins,
unworthy to feel this love and affection
of which sacredly I hold for You,
accept O Lord this offering
of my heart and soul
surrendering to You my all.

The 1st Week of Lent

Day 8, Wednesday – Prayer for World Peace

"I will seek that which was lost, and bring again that which was driven away, and will bind up that which was broken, and will strengthen that which was sick: but I will destroy the fat and the strong; I will feed them with judgment."[13]

Great Father, whose power abounds mightily, let Your mercy be upon us for our world is inclined on violence and destruction. Aggression and oppression are upon the innocent. Father, forgive us, awaken our souls who live in darkness to let Your light and peace come into our hearts. Transform our souls to turn to You and grant us a new life with You in it.

O Beloved Jesus, govern and raise us up as You had done before. "In indignation You marched through the earth; In anger You trampled the nations. You went forth for the salvation of Your people, For the salvation of Your anointed. You struck the head of the house of the evil to lay him open from thigh to neck....." [14] Deign O Jesus to save us.

O Holy Spirit, create a pure heart in all of us. Grant us to walk with a loyal spirit towards You. O most Holy Trinity, wherein love and wisdom shine, the light of the living, come have mercy on us, grant us peace.

*The love of Jesus is around us, love Him
and love will go around.*

---

13 Ezekiel 34:16
14 Habakkuk 3:12

Meditation

We're bewildered and dismayed
in this crumbling world of ours
where we ought to live in harmony
not in fear nor anger.
Our souls ought to radiate light
not hide in darkness;
we've squandered Your Grace
Lord behold us.

We turn to You with sighs and tears,
end the shaking and trembling,
protect us from our assailants
and make earth a place of worship.
Lord, teach us to forgive one another
that we may walk together united as one
so that we may fulfill Your intent for us
to love one another as You have loved us.

The 1ˢᵗ Week of Lent

Day 9, Thursday – Ask Virgin Mary to Pray for Us

"Behold, a Virgin shall conceive and bear a son;
and his name will be called Emmanuel."[15]

Mother Mary, you who experienced great sorrow in your own life here on earth for the love of Your Son, and you who show love and compassion to all your children, pray for me, my family, my friends and relatives, and all my brothers and sisters who are in the midst of their own trials and tribulations. Heavenly mother, you know your children's sufferings, hopes and desires, you also know our struggle with the enemy in this world, hear our cry and intercede with our prayers as we consecrate our world to You.

From your grace, O gentle lady, may we live intimately close to You: humble us, move us, and gentle us above the perplexities of our life here on earth. Pray for us to be purified and completely cleansed so that we may be blessed by Your Son to aspire for the joy that comes from becoming faithful witnesses to Him, our Lord and Savior, Jesus Christ.

God greatly blest Virgin Mary from her mother's
womb because she is to be very special,
she is to become the Mother of His Son!

---

15 Isaiah 7:14

Meditation

Happy are they who know
the love of Mother Mary
whom the Holy Spirit had blest.
Gentle Spirit, bless us to be under
the loving care of our glorious Patroness.

O blessed Mother who nourished baby Jesus
and brought Him up to manhood,
you who forever nourish babes in heaven
with your gentle hands and motherly care,
assist us.

Pray for us, O loving Mother in heaven,
engage us to be among God's people
to be fostered as newborns
without stain, raised and restored
so as to be called the sons and daughters
of the Most High.

The 1st Week of Lent

Day 10, Friday – Desire Charity to Serve Others

"If I give all I possess to the poor and give over my body to hardship that I may boast, but do not have love, I gain nothing."[16]

God of love, Your St. Paul stated that charity should begin with oneself. It is of no value if we give all that we possess but have no love. Lord, fill my heart with love for others in need in order for me to be grounded in charity and for my soul to produce fruits of grace. Grant me strength and courage that I may serve with all my will. Bless my heart to feel the love for many especially the poor and the sick, and let these desires of my heart be forever that I may delight You as long as I live in order to yield for You glory and praise the rest of my life.

May you grant all of us to help one another with love, not for selfish reasons as your St. Matthew wrote *(Jesus speaking)*: "Beware of practicing your righteousness before other people in order to be seen by them, for then you will have no reward from your Father who is in heaven. Thus, when you give to the needy, sound no trumpet before you, as the hypocrites do in the synagogues and in the streets, that they may be praised by others. Truly, I say to you, they

---

16 1 Corinthians 13:3

have received their reward. But when you give to the needy, do not let your left hand know what your right hand is doing, so that your giving may be in secret. And your Father who sees in secret will reward you."[17]

*What great grace it is for God to allow His intercessions
in our undeserving hearts and souls.*

17 Matthew 6:1-4

Meditation

Deny self –
If anyone wants to follow in His footsteps
give up all right to himself;
Sell all possessions and
distribute them to the poor.

Renounce everything –
How extremely difficult to do
for us mere humans
yet extremely rewarding
for treasure will be in heaven.

Lord Jesus –
whose heart flamed by fire
consumed Your saints to follow You.
Come and enkindle in my heart
that delightful flame
that I may deny myself and follow You.

The 1st Week of Lent

Day 11, Saturday – Prayer for our Children

*"I tell you the truth, unless you change and become like
little children, you will never enter the kingdom of heaven.
Therefore, whoever humbles himself like this child is the
greatest in the kingdom of heaven. "And whoever
welcomes a little child like this in my name welcomes me.
But if anyone causes one of these little ones who believe in
me to sin, it would be better for him to have a large
millstone hung around his neck and to be drowned
in the depths of the sea. "[18]*

Thank you Father for the gifts of little children. May they
grow strong and healthy: physically, mentally, emotionally
and spiritually, and be guided by the Holy Spirit. May their
parents and caretakers also be guided to bring them up with
their most tender love and care.

Blessed Saviour, we thank You for the children of our time
who have followed Your guidance. Bless their hearts who
are completely drawn to You and who are righteous in Your
eyes. May You continue to bless them that they may stay
true and faithful to You to the end.

Thank You Lord for precious little children and the faithful
ones. Currently, we are faced with other children who have
not followed Your guidance. Give us strength to endure as
we face the rising problems of disobedience, drugs, alcohol

---

18 Matthew 18:2-6

and distrust on others. For some, life has outgrown trust, faith, hope and miracles. Help us continue to extend our unswerving love to our children even in the midst of our emotional pain and sorrow toward those who neglect You, those who do not believe in You, and those who have other Gods. Help these innocent victims who have become defiant. Soften their hearts to You; make their spiritual eyes to see, their ears to hear and hearts to come to You, I pray O loving Savior, help us and our children.

*May the Lord bless our children with His light and
wisdom as we bow in humility before Him.*

Meditation

Despite our sins
You bless and forgive us.
You never fail to show us Your love,
You even bless us in so many ways
that we can never repay You.

Thank You Lord
for all Your goodness,
for the gifts of sons and daughters
and for the precious little ones like
our grandchildren and great-grandchildren.

Bless them Father,
grant them to be free from harm:
physically, emotionally and spiritually.
Bless them to grow in grace with faith.
Grant that we may be good parents
and grandparents guided by Your Spirit.

The 2nd Week of Lent

Day 12, Second Sunday – Surrender All

"Let every soul be subject unto the higher powers.
For there is no power but of God: the powers that be
are ordained of God."[19]

O most gracious Lord and Maker to whom I owe the gift of my present life. I am poor and weak but You have blessed me with all that I have and all that I am. I come to You my loving Father to do Your command, do with me as You please for You are my God who loves me.

Father, here is my heart, take it for I give You all of the love it can hold. Receive O loving God my freedom, my capability and my identification. Use the little time I have left in this world, my every breath and my every strength that You have graciously blessed me with to labor for Your glory, and let me not do anything for myself for I want You to take all of me to do Your divine will for I surrender all that You've given me, back to You.

I will live for You and serve You until the time when You will let me live with You forever I pray, with Your blessed Son Jesus in the heavenly kingdom, in whose holiest name I pray. Amen.

There is another world out there worth surrendering to,
that is full of light and life!

---

19 Romans 13:1

Meditation

*I am poor, born with nothing
and most content with my life
for the grace of the Lord
is all I need.*

*I have no precious gifts to give
neither gold nor silver to offer Him
only this poor heart of mine
filled with love for Him.*

*His heart is pure and true
His love is most sincere
His Words are my bond
He is my Salvation.*

*Therefore, I will live this life
desiring nothing for myself
nor from anyone
except to do His Will.*

The 2nd Week of Lent

Day 13, Monday – Thank God for His Sacrament

"... and when He had given thanks, He broke it and said, "This is My body, which is for you; do this in remembrance of Me." In the same way He took the cup also after supper, saying, "This cup is the new covenant in My Blood; do this, as often as you drink it, in remembrance of Me."[20]

God of my life, in atonement for my failures, I come to You on bended knees, look down upon this feeble soul of the earth who praise you with thanksgiving for the blessed opportunity to be among Your children to receive Your holy Body and Blood through the Sacrament.

Lord Jesus, thank You for Your never-ending love, that even now after two thousand years, You still love us offering Your holy Body where You hide Your splendor. Shrunk and broken into pieces of bread You allow us to touch You with our unclean hands to be swallowed inside our throats that partaking in this sacred communion, we may be cleansed by Your divine mystery. Forgive us Jesus. You sunk Your highness to its lowest point for us. Thank You O loving Lord, thank You most kindly for Your great and undying love. Honored and blessed are they who reverently receive Your Body and Blood for You our Lord Jesus Christ is the name to bless, worship and pray to, our Lamb who takes away the sins of the world. Amen.

To know God's truth is simply to turn the pages of the Bible. May we not turn away from Him.

---

20 1 Corinthians 11:24-25

Meditation

Adoring Your wondrous grace,
the heart of my tongue is eager
and anxious is my soul to approach You.
By Your loving grace, my thirst and hunger
would be satisfied once we consummate.

How sweet is Your sacrament
where truly You are present
not only in the breaking of the bread
for You are the bread Itself, You Who
also give strength to our body and soul.

May all thirst and hunger
to receive Your holy Body and Blood
in the sacrament of holy communion.
May Your blessed grace continue to spread
throughout our world without end.

The 2nd Week of Lent

Day 14, Tuesday – Prayer for Churches

"One thing have I desired of the LORD, that will I seek after; that I may dwell in the house of the LORD all the days of my life, to behold the beauty of the LORD, and to inquire in his temple."[21]

Lord Almighty, we who believe cherish the divine atmosphere of Your holy church wherein Your holy fragrance surrounds, where we seek You to cast ourselves into Your arms that we may dwell with You to behold the joy of You and be sheltered by Your holy church as we bow our heads to pray. Bless all Your church around the world O great God that they may be protected as we continue to praise and bless You within their walls. Prosper them along with Your devoted priests, ministers and holy religious who are devoutly working for Your honor and glory. Bless them with pure hearts, make them humble and faithful to their duty til their last breath.

O righteous God who rescued His people from the hands of their enemies in the times of David, Saul, Joshua and all the other Kings, build us a strong fortress and rescue us from the power of the enemy. Support Your churches and children from the cruelties of merciless persecutors, and make our world be still, not stormy. Under the roofs of Your

---

21 Psalm 27.4

bride, grant Your churches peace. Grant our Christian devotion to be duly maintained by Your bounty as we continue to witness, spread Your Word, sanctify Your name, and worship You Father, our peacemaker, the power of all strength, through Jesus Christ our Lord, I pray. Amen.

Giving up ourselves tenderly to Jesus would make him
rejoice as he tenderly caress our lives.

Meditation

All churches and its followers
throughout the world
confess that You are the Father
of heaven and earth
who shine forth Your light forever.

Life of all life, save us.
Defeat the enemy, restore our temples,
renew our confidence, beliefs and faith,
raise us all up to be Your steeples
and pillars of the earth.

O mighty defender
lead our way in quiet freedom,
pardon us and direct our feet
into the way of peace through Christ
to whom all glory, honor and worship
be now and always.

The 2nd Week of Lent

Day 15, Wednesday – Praise God

"Yours, O LORD, is the greatness and the power and the glory and the majesty and the splendor, for everything in heaven and earth is yours. Yours, LORD, is the kingdom; you are exalted as head over all."[22]

O God of my life, unworthy as I am who do not deserve anything much more Your love, allow me to praise You and give You thanks for Your blessedness. Blessed are You who breathe life into us, and into our hearts You make a dwelling place. I praise You O great almighty Creator for Your power and greatness. The thrill of winds, thunderstorms and hail come and go at Your command. The murmur of the waves, the rushing river, and the calmness of the woods, You make to be all soothing to our ears. The moon You make to come softly in the night as You whisper it to stay and the sun You make to appear to bring us day. You have set the majesty of the mountain range, its height and depth, the ocean's floor and all the foundation of the universe and the earth for You are God, our great eternal God.

As one little speck of dust You have created who is most unworthy to even speak of You and of Your Greatness, I humbly praise You and thank You most lovingly to be among Your fortunate creation to be surrounded by Your

---

22 1 Chronicles 29:11

nature's beauty. Thank you Lord God for Your magnificent creation. I exalt You for all the countless blessings You have provided me and for all of us for we depend on You, we depend on Your world and Your mercy, but most of all we depend on Your love.

Love Jesus like no one has, and please the Father like never before.

Meditation

In hot or winter days,
in solitude or crowded place
You're there present in our midst.
Your radiance brings sparks in our lives
Your bright light opens the hearts of our eyes
And Your love is as the sun breathing life into us.
We need Your love O Lord as we need air above the sky.

You feed our hunger
and refresh our thirsty souls.
You give us bread and wine to drink
You bring us priests, nuns and mystics too,
and never fail to lavish us with nature's gifts.
O source of all life, the sole essence of all beings
To whom ever should we lean on if not for You, my God?

The 2nd Week of Lent

Day 16, Thursday – Pray To Rescue Us

"The Lord is my light and my salvation Whom shall I fear?
The Lord is the defense of my life; Whom shall I dread."[23]

Father, may every dormant soul be awakened from their sleep to hear Your voice, see Your countenance and delight in the spirit of Your love. O what a joyful world we'd be in if only all would believe in Your truth, Your Son Jesus Christ. Deliver us from transgressors and persecutors. Forgive us for no doubt we have reached our peak of sinfulness. Lord, pity the entrapped souls that long for Your peace, Your love and Your presence within.

In despair, may we all cry out to You O forgiving Father. Rescue us from threats and dangers of our sins that we may survive the storms of our world. With Your power, save us by Your deliverance, grant Your Holy Spirit to descend upon us all to praise You, serve You and love You in order to end hostilities, as the writer of the Epistle said: "Let us lay aside the works of darkness, and put on the armor or light. Let us walk becomingly as in the day, not in revelry and drunkenness, not in debauchery and wantonness, not in strife and jealousy. But put on the Lord Jesus Christ."[24] O God of life, in Your beloved and blessed name Lord Jesus, I kneel and pray. Amen.

We need rescue from ourselves, but who is there
to rescue us but God?

---

23 Psalm 27:1
24 Epistle – Rom. 13:12-14

Meditation

O Lord,
we cry out to You.
The clouds are above us,
and the wind is blowing strong,
shaking us, trembling our souls,
we hear the weeping with great grief.

Great One,
rescue us from this
mad world where abuse and
injustice are done to those who believe.
Let Your peace come to hearts that are cold
and hardened, and souls overcomed by violence.

God of power,
You hate wickedness,
You will destroy the evildoers.
Although you bring us grief now
You also show us compassion always
You will never forsake us for You are our
Lord, Our God, our light and our salvation.

The 2nd Week of Lent

Day 17, Friday – Strive to Become Spiritual

"Behold, you delight in truth in the inward being, and you teach me wisdom in the secret heart."[25]

God Almighty, comfort and strengthen me to be able to commit to Your will. Let me not be eager to know what my future holds, but rather let me be eager to know what Your will is for me as I try to amend my life. Bless me to be more passionate in my spiritual progress to allow me to labor now. I do not consider myself secured in any way, but I will be firm in my hope to succeed in this life in my walk with You. I will continue to be vigilant and diligent by Your grace in my service to You, both physically and spiritually.

Help me to speak little, rise early, eat sparingly, read more religiously, spend more time in prayer, listen to Your words and keep disciplined at all times. Let me not rejoice in the comfort of the eyes and body or anything created by this world, rather let me rejoice in the days and nights that I spend profitably with You. Grant me to do all the above Lord because I can't do them alone without You. Through my thoughts, through my service and through my prayers, in Christ name by whom all glory and honor be forever I pray. Amen.

How little time remains for us on earth; may we abandon the little time we have left completely to His will.

---

25 Psalm 51:6

Meditation

O quiet friend,
source of all creation,
fountain of everlasting light,
mighty and eternal are You yet
mysteriously you make abode
within our unholy hearts.

Gently, You come in
to us, sweetly saying: If a man
love me, he will keep my Word,
and my Father will love him, and
we will come in to him, and we will
make our abode with him. "[26]

Bless me Lord to give
attention only to my interior
for to seek richness and comfort
other than Your love would
for certain impede my
spiritual growth.

Lord, bestow within me
obedience, lowliness, humility
and charity that I may contemplate
heavenly things to hopefully by Your
grace, I may frequently feel the
joy of heaven here on earth
as it is in heaven.

---

26 John 15:23

The 2nd Week of Lent

Day 18, Saturday – Ask to be God's Instrument

"You are the salt of the earth; but if salt has lost its taste, how can its saltiness be restored? It is no longer good for anything, but is thrown out and trampled under foot."[27]

Father, origin of all that is good, bless me to be an instrument of Your love. Grant me the power to understand and to undertake the responsibility of being a good servant. Open my heart and soul that I may not only see but feel the need of others. Grant me to help those who have lost their way in order to be restored back to You, and teach me to be able to bring hope, comfort and joy to those who suffer and grieve.

Lord God, though I may never ever be fit to be made as Your instrument of love, I pray to bless me with a heart and soul open and ready to share with all who needs help. Bless me to do what I have to do not desiring anything back in return, nor resisting anything back from You my Lord, to whom I serve, to whom be all honor and glory here on earth and in heaven, in Jesus name. Amen.

May we value His free gift of love,
and allow Him to love us freely.

---

27 Matthew 5:13-16

Meditation

Lord, Uncreated,
Maker of all created things,
whose glory is incomprehensible,
whose might is inconceivable
and whose mercy is immeasurable,
what return could I give You,
You whose presence is with us infinitely
and who endlessly grant us life?

Let me open my heart to You O God
and fill it with utmost desire to serve.
Grant me to pledge a loyal service
to forego this earthly life as an instrument
of Your never-ending work of healing
and redemption of mankind,
all for You O great One, through whom
all glory and honor be for all eternity.

The 3rd Week of Lent

Day 19, Third Sunday – Soul Cleansing

"I will sprinkle clean water on you, and you will be clean; I will cleanse you from all your impurities and from all your idols. I will give you a new heart and put a new spirit in you; I will remove from you your heart of stone and give you a heart of flesh. And I will put my Spirit in you and move you to follow my decrees and be careful to keep my laws."[28]

Heavenly Father, enlighten our soul on the things that have been written and spoken so that we sinners will know not only the truth of Your Word but also obey Your rules and commandments, that we may become spiritual people working together to reach our goal to have eternal life with You in heaven.

Grant us Lord of heaven Your forgiveness for all the sins we commit day and night, in words, thoughts and actions. Bless us all to make amends and continue to worship You day in and day out the rest of our lives. Take away from us all evil inclinations, our impurities, our pride, covetousness and all vain glory. Make us free from envy, deceit, falsehood, lust, sloth and all kinds of malice, and break our souls from hypocrisy, anger and wrath. Lord, may You sanctify our souls in order for our bodies and spirits to be cleansed and purified by Your love.

The time of life is short; if we hold life dear and believe,
life will be forever in God's Kingdom.

---

28 Ezekiel 36:25

Meditation

Blessed Master
help our souls desiring
to be cleansed and purified.
Wash our sins within us hoping
to be rinsed of dirt and defilement.
Touch us for You're the one who could
extract from our hearts and souls sinning.

Purge us Lord
with hyssop wanting
to be forgiven and praying
to be cured with souls singing
and at last washed, and enlightened.
Come O blessed Lord, come we all pray
Give us a new heart and put a new spirit in us.
Renew us all as our hearts dance with joy loving.

The 3rd Week of Lent

Day 20, Monday – Honor God

"Arise, O God, judge the earth for thou
shalt inherit all nations."[29]

Dear Father I come to You not to ask as I normally do, I come not to beg nor plead as I often do, but I come to honor You because I believe in You for You are our true God. I have faith in You for You give me comfort and blessings. I trust in You for Your Words are true, I hope in You for You are everlasting, and I give You glory for You are my God who gives salvation.

Lord Jesus, our gentle Savior, I rejoice in You. I love that I know You, I love Your inconceivable love for all and Your immeasurable mercy. I will praise Your name all the rest of my life. To Your name Lord Jesus, be all the glory, honor and worship til the end of time.

O Holy Spirit, our Star and Guide, You who infuse grace into our souls, You who make hearts shine, I praise You, Your infinite wisdom, Your guidance and Your primal light. I will praise You without ceasing. To the Father, the Son and the Holy Spirit I pray. Amen.

This above all, to God be faithful til death,
for God is faithful til our end.

29 Psalm 82:8

Meditation

*How precious is Your name
O Holy One, Friend of my heart
whose everlasting kingdom
and dominion endures forever.
I glorify Your majesty, I extol Your
wondrous work of hands.*

*Your love endures forever
Your strength and power sustains
O Prince of the universe
Lord of all, watch over us
for we trust in You.*

*Let my tongue praise You
as I bow my head to my waist.
Receive my thanks O Life of my life,
come O King of kings,
come and rule our world
always and forever.*

The 3rd Week of Lent

Day 21, Tuesday – Humble Contrition

"The LORD is near to the brokenhearted
And saves those who are crushed in spirit."[30]

Almighty and Everlasting God, I'm not worthy of Your compassion and consolation. My sorrowful regret for my sins is not an acceptable sacrifice but I pray that my tears, prayers, meditations, sorrows and service I offer including but not the least, my most fervent love for You may be acceptable in Your sight. Father, grant my mind, body and soul full remission of all my sins that I may walk in the way of Your love. Grant all of us to walk in love as Your St. Paul said: "Therefore be imitators of God, as beloved children. And walk in love, as Christ loved us and gave himself up for us, a fragrant offering and sacrifice to God".

Lord of my life, I pray that my humble act of contrition, daily Lent offering of prayers, penance and thanksgiving be pleasing to You granting that I may not fail to do Your will. Let whatever You will for me be infused deep in my heart and soul that I may serve truly and faithfully and love You the Father, Your Son and the Holy Spirit forever and ever. Amen.

May our hearts love Him more than the soul
of our love could give.

---

30 Psalm 34:18

Meditation

Merciful God,
origin of all good.
I'm poor in spirit and heart,
one unworthy of Your forgiving,
I seek Your grace to grant me Your blessing.

Lead my soul
to seek no part of anything,
for my own selfish pleasure
for nothing would please You well
as to be completely humble and gentle.

Help me O Lord
to forsake what is appealing
that I may see them rather appalling.
Shield me from worldly and mortal desires
and grant me I pray to desire for perfect humility.

The 3rd Week in Lent

Day 22, Wednesday – Rejoice in His Love

"Rejoice in the Lord always. I will say it again: Rejoice!"[31]

Beloved Love, Your love is so great that only You could define it. Through our waking years You make our love grow: may they be in gladness, sadness, darkness, rain or shine, it grows and endures. God forever blessed, Your love always remains the same, You are kind and patient, and Your grace is always sufficient. Grant our unworthy souls to rejoice in You. You are a reason to rejoice even in times of sickness, emotional distress, affliction or persecution for You are in the midst of us, we who believe and hope in You for Your love always speaks of our peace, pardon and salvation.

Thank You Almighty Father for your mercy and grace upon us. Bless and save our souls from all falsity of this life to allow our hearts to rejoice in Your perfect love. All praise to You O Father and Your Son with the Holy Spirit. All honor and glory be to the sacred name of our Lord Jesus Christ forever and ever. Amen.

It's hard to believe God's love. Who would believe that someday we'll see heaven? We only have to believe to see.

---

31 Philippians 4:4

Meditation

I am grateful
O Lord for my life
for the joys and peace
for the failures and successes
but mostly the love from You O God.

You seasoned my life
with such delight as the sun,
moon, summer air and winter snow,
the blue sky, the green grass of summer
and all the splendored things of the world.

Thank You Lord
for Your gifts of grace,
from the love of family and friends
even in times of sadness, good or bad,
You touch our lives in so many special ways.

The 3rd Week in Lent

Day 23, Thursday – Pray in Times of Trouble

"Finally, be strong in the Lord and in the strength of his might. Put on the whole armor of God, that you may be able to stand against the schemes of the devil. For we do not wrestle against flesh and blood, but against the rulers, against the authorities, against the cosmic powers over this present darkness, against the spiritual forces of evil in the heavenly places. Therefore take up the whole armor of God that you may be able to withstand in the evil day, and having done all, to stand firm"[32]

O Mighty God, we don't know what to do when things are not well with us except to run to You for we rely on Your strength and power in times of trouble. There are times when we succumb to our wickedness and give in to temptations. We are feeble, unable to help ourselves or heal our weaknesses. God of power, seal us from the enemy: hide us from all kinds of temptations; the enemies' trickeries; and our own misleading fears. Give us strength to avoid the deceit of false spirits who roam around our world whose sole purpose is to ruin our souls. Lord, we trust and hope in Your loving kindness and mercy.

Lord God, my Guide and Protector, I commend all the needs of my body and soul to You. I entrust my whole self, my

---

32 Ephesians 6:10-18

family, my friends, relatives, neighbors, and brothers and sisters to You, protect us from all kinds of evil. In the most blessed name of Jesus I pray. Amen.

Pray and endure when suffering comes for nothing is more acceptable to God than to suffer for Him willingly.

Meditation

O mighty God,
what a comfort it is to know
that we could come to You
through our fears, grief and sorrows;
that through the depths of our sufferings
You help us bear and endure
for You are our strength.

Protect us against the evil of the unseen world
who tries to afflict our minds when we're weary.
Let all evil pass us by as You did Your saints
who had many temptations and tribulations,
but passed through their sufferings
and even profited with the
protection of Your love.

We would endure our affliction
"For You are faithful;
You will not let us be tempted
beyond that which we are able to bear,
but with the temptation will also make a way
to escape, that we may be able to bear it."[33]
Lord God, make us strong.

---

33 Corinthians 10:13

The 3rd Week of Lent

Day 24, Friday – Follow the Cross

"Then Jesus told his disciples, "If anyone would come after me, let him deny himself and take up his cross and follow me. For whoever would save his life will lose it, but whoever loses his life for my sake will find it. For what will it profit a man if he gains the whole world and forfeits his soul?"[34]

O good and merciful God, let not our faith flicker and faint, nor our minds wander off here and there. May we all resolve to read the Bible and understand it especially the part of Your Son's passion, for us to take up our cross and follow Him, "for we know that our old self was crucified with him so that the body ruled by sin might be done away with, that we should no longer be slaves to sin."[35]

Since sin dwells in us at the present time for we ourselves are the prime cause of our miseries, grant our souls to seek repentance to be restored in order to have an everlasting life with You who give everlasting reward to those who labor without end for Your honor and glory. O blessed Father, absolve us from all our inequities, deliver us from the bond of all evil. By the love, passion and death of Your beloved Son, our Lord and Savior Jesus Christ I pray. Amen.

There is a difference between good and bad.
May we be able to distinguish good from evil.

---

34 Matthew 16:24-25
35 Romans 6:6

Meditation

For us a child was born
through a virgin created.
He is God's only begotten Son
who led a perfect life full of mystery.
His sacred passion shook the earth
and His death baffled the world.

His life and death reached all souls,
faithful hearts felt His loving presence
and with His precious Blood
He triumphed over sin
revealing His saving power
to the ends of the earth.

Lord, open the chambers of my heart;
receive it and guide the root of its soul
for I no longer wish to lead it myself.
Allow me to follow You from hereon
that I may someday enter heaven into the joys
of Your loving arms.

The 3rd Week in Lent

Day 25, Saturday – Enter in the Presence of the Spirit

"Praise be to the God and Father of our Lord Jesus Christ, who has blessed us in the heavenly realms with every spiritual blessing in Christ."[36]

Blessed Jesus, teach us to take the spiritual path to journey with You through solitude. Through complete silence, we can learn to be still, our souls can open up to You, we can talk to You, and hope for Your Spirit to come near us or hopefully dwell in our hearts to feel Your loving presence and to maybe even hear Your sweet voice as we commune with You through solemn prayers.

As Your St. Paul wrote: "For this reason I bow my knees before the Father from whom every family in heaven and on earth takes its name. I pray that, according to the riches of the glory, he may grant that you may be strengthened in your inner being power through his Spirit, and that Christ may dwell in your hearts through faith, as you are being rooted and grounded in love. I pray that you may have the power to comprehend, with all the saints, what is the breadth and length and height and depth, and to know the love of Christ that surpasses knowledge, so that you may be filled

---

36 Ephesians 1:3

with the fullness of God. Now to him who by the power at work within us is able to accomplish abundantly far more than all we can ask or imagine, to him be glory in the church and in Christ Jesus to all generations forever and ever. Amen."[37]

Our world is full of life with troubles and difficulties, but if we embrace them with full spirit, we'll live a glorious life after.

37 Ephesians 3:14-21

Meditation

Father, holy and true,
so loving and so kind,
my grateful heart sings to You
as I praise You each morn
and thank You at each close of day.

O gentle Spirit,
whose voice I hear in the wind,
whose breath gives life to the world,
fill my soul with Your Holy Spirit
as I commune with You in solitude.

Lift me up I pray,
reveal Your beauty deep in my soul
that I may find You and Your love divine
dwelling in my longing heart
in the silence of the night.

Blessed Jesus,
Cleanse me by Your sacred mysteries
for my spirit to be anewed
that I may, in complete silence of my soul
be filled with the fullness of You.

The 4ᵗʰ Week of Lent

Day 26, Fourth Sunday – Venerate the Blessed Virgin

"The angel answered, "The Holy Spirit will come to you, and the power of the Most High will overshadow you. So the holy one to be born will be called the Son of God."[38]

O blessed Virgin, created to perfection, you have appeared on earth numerous times and many looked to you for protection and honored you for generations. People looked on you as the Virgin conceived without sin and through centuries your words have been fulfilled in many ways. Blessed, Immaculate and Patroness are just a few names we give to honor you for all that you have done for us. In return, we should love you as St. John, the disciple said: "Love for Mary will draw us close to Jesus."[39]

May all see your blessedness. May all trust and respect you totally and give you the reverence you deserve for you were, beyond our imagination and comprehension, created and designed for a purpose, the bride of the Holy Spirit, Queen of heaven, mother of church, bride of the Father and mostly the mother of God!

O glorious sweet bride of heaven, forgive us for adding sorrow to your holy heart. I humbly ask for you to pray for tepid souls and give knowledge to the innocent who refuse

---

38 Luke 1:35
39 John 2:5

to know you with the blessings of your truth. May they come to console you for their ingratitude that bring forth thorns to your heart. May they venerate your blessed name and place a crown in your immaculate heart for God Himself has done great things for you, as you stated: "My soul proclaims the greatness of the Lord, my spirit rejoices in God my Savior for he has looked with favor on His lowly servant."[40]

Virgin Mary committed herself to God.
He will work within us when we commit to Him.

40 Luke 1:46

Meditation

Virgin Mary, holy and pure
conceived by divine wisdom,
sanctified before you were born,
was blest in your mother's womb.

Embrace us with your simple charm,
you who bring sweet joys into souls
inspiring us to imitate your virtues,
hold our hands and walk with us.

You are filled with God's gifts,
behold our poor spirits with love
and affection to our poor souls
for us to yearn for your holiness.

Let us feel your peace,
oblige purity deep in our hearts.
Help us O mother in heaven,
hear us for we need you in this life.

The 4th Week of Lent

Day 27, Monday – Return God's Love

"Hear, O Israel: The LORD our God, the LORD is one.
Love the LORD your God with all your heart and with all
your soul and with all your strength."[41]

Father, innumerable times we've stated that there would be no living things in the universe, no fowls of the air nor beasts of the earth, no sun or moon, nor day or night without You who out of love had ordained for this perfect world to exist solely for the creatures You made. Your unspeakable providence is so incredulous it is unimaginable how some of us have yet to see and understand Your undying love. Despite Your greatness, You are compassionate, faithful and ever so loving even when we have become disobedient. How could we be so blind to Your proof of love? How could we ignore the truth? Yet no matter what we've become You continue to provide for us. You nourish us day by day. This is why Your Son said: "For this reason I say to you, do not be worried about your life, as to what you will eat or what you will drink; nor for your body, as to what you will put on. Is not life more than food, and the body more than clothing? Look at the birds of the air, that they do not sow, nor reap nor gather into barns, and yet your heavenly Father feeds them. Are you not worth much more than they?"[42]

41 Deuteronomy 6:4-5
42 Matthew 6:25-26

Lord God, let us not be worried about ourselves but rather let us pray that we may have time to show You our gratitude and faithfulness. Create in each of us a heart filled with infinite love so that we may be able to return Your love as immensely as we could. Let us not perish but allow us to produce new roots, make us shine and bloom again like the plants and flowers, together with all the fowls of the air and beasts of the earth in order that we may have life with You in Your heavenly kingdom for all eternity, in Jesus' name I pray.

I give myself entirely back to You, who created me,
with all of my heart's love and affection.

Meditation

Passion.
To prove Your love caused You
to descend to the lowest of Yourself
for that's when Your love is strongest.
How could we be so blind to Your love?

The Lamb.
Not even the slightest humiliation
nor a single drop of Your precious Blood
should be sacrificed for our eternal sin.
Was there no other way, O Lord?

Love.
Your love is boundless,
You keep giving Your all to ungrateful men.
Don't even birds sing You melodies, and
flowers exhume their fragrance to You?

Behold.
God from heaven declared:
'This is my Beloved Son,
with whom I am well pleased.'
Should we ignore this truth?

Jesus,
on your return,
there shall be joy, there will be singing
and every knee will bow before You,
for every tongue will acknowledge You
as God!

The 4th Week of Lent

Day 28, Tuesday – Pray for Holiness

"Therefore, since we have these promises, dear friends, let us purify ourselves from everything that contaminates body and spirit, perfecting holiness out of reverence for God." [43]

Grace me O God to receive the light of understanding from above that I may have a pure, simple and steady spirit. May my interior walk with You be performed to honor and glorify Your name, with not the slightest thought of the exterior freeing myself from any self-seeking desires. Remembering what Solomon said that: "the eye is not satisfied with seeing, nor is the ear filled with hearing"[44] that all things are full of weariness, all things come and go. Everything will pass away but You remain the same, Your love is sweet, kind, patient, understanding, unselfish, priceless, and eternal.

Father, help me to withdraw my heart from the love of all visible things that I may not lose sight of Your love and Your grace. Let my soul to look ahead with hope, my heart with joy and my mind reposed in You peaceably that I may grow with You in holiness, through the grace of Your Son Jesus Christ. Amen.

God's voice may be a whisper from the interior,
but it's power is loud and clear.
May we be blest with ears to hear His Words.

---

43 2 Corinthians 7:1
44 Ecclesiastes 1:8

Meditation

We offend You
when the sun rises
or when the moon sets at dawn.
We sin against You
by thought, word or deed
intentionally or inadvertently,
generation after generation
we remain the same.

Yet You my God,
You do not leave us.
You seek us and look after us
generation after generation,
You remain the same.
Let us make amends O God,
let the love of the faithful
make up for the rest.

When the sun shines
let all sing You songs.
When the moon rises
let all praise Your name
and proclaim Your Glory.
Purify us Lord, make us holy
and let us remain this way
generation after generation.

The 4th Week of Lent

Day 29, Wednesday – Focus on God Alone

"Set your minds on things that are above,
not on things that are on earth."[45]

Lord Jesus, grant me the compunction of heart to give You my whole devotion granting me no distractions that I may not lose my daily focus on You. Grant me no acknowledgment to my small self but only to You, Your holiness and divineness at all times. Let me have the fear of You when I sin and the happiness when I feel Your solid joy. I pray that I may not busy myself on other things when I ought to attend to Your calling, rather only be concerned with the work You give me to do and may I be blessed to do them well.

Humbly I pray O Lord Jesus to give me a spirit focused only on You as I try to work my way to doing well in serving You. Help me to find no difficulty in resisting temptations in order to be successful in my walk with You interiorly and exteriorly. May You grant my heart to aspire, hunger and thirst for You that I may live to serve only You, my Master, My Lord my God. Amen.

Let us contemplate on our future – in heaven,
our eternal home where Jesus is.

---

45 Colossians 3:2

Meditation

There's no eternity
no winds nor waves,
no heaven and earth,
below, above and everywhere
without You,
for all force of nature
surrender to You.

And I, a tiny speck of dust,
aware that everyday life
is under Your control
will soon decease.
Bless me loving Jesus
while there is time
to fix my eyes on You alone.

The 4th Week of Lent

Day 30, Thursday – Prayer for the Gifts of the Spirit

*"But the manifestation of the Spirit is given to
every man to profit withal."* [46]

Faithful God, thank You for blessing us who do not deserve anything. Thank You for Your Son who came down in human form into our lives, and in spiritual form into our hearts. In Your extreme love for us You allowed Him to die to be reconciled with us, and graced us further with Your Holy Spirit. May Your Spirit living within us enlighten our hearts so that we may show You an ever faithful love You deserve.

Before You O great Spirit of God, I kneel to offer my whole self, body and soul. You are the light of my soul, the strength of my heart, and the love of my life. Bless me to keep my eyes focused on You, my ears to listen to Your voice, and my soul to follow You, Your light and guidance. Watch over me and my loved ones, help us when we are sick, guard over us when we are weak, keep us away from any harm, physically, mentally, emotionally and spiritually. Be our light all the rest of our lives. Grant that we may never sin against You O Holy Spirit of God, by the grace and love of Your Son Jesus Christ, I pray. Amen.

*Knowing He can do anything, once in a while,
I ask Him what I can do for Him.*

---

46 1 Corinthians 12:7-11

Meditation

Guest of my soul,
O sweet Spirit of God
Whose glory shines forever,
so bright, so divine, it never fails.
I call upon You O glorious Holy Spirit
to thank You for lingering over us humans,
we who are enslaved by sins.
Thank You for your endless light,
thank you for your tender love and care.

O gentle Spirit of God,
flourish us with gifts.
Grant us wisdom to know good from evil,
understanding to enlighten our minds,
counsel that we may be righteous,
knowledge to know Your love,
fortitude to have courage to fight the enemy,
piety to acquire compassionate hearts,
fear to draw back from evil,
and submit to what is good.

The 4th Week of Lent

Day 31, Friday – Prayer on Relationships

"That thou mayst walk in a good way:
and mayst keep the paths of the just."[47]

Loving God, You designed us not to live alone but to live with one another. We are grateful for friends and families for they are gifts from You. As time goes by, we become close to each other, we learn to love and value friends and neighbors, but there are times when we don't relate to each other causing us to break relationships or worst, become enemies.

Forgive us Lord for our flaws, forgive our faults due to our selfish behavior. For even though we try our best to save a friendship, we sometimes simply fail. Help us Lord to learn how to keep a healthy relationship with one another. Bless us Lord to learn how to respond to one another when problems arise. Bless us to be grateful for one another. Grant us to be thankful for good friends, to be truthful to each other, to be unselfish and loyal as friendship is important to You as our friendship to You is most important to us. Grant us to live our lives loving one another.

Examination of self is healthy to make things
right with self and one another.

---

47 Proverbs 2:20

Meditation

"1 The proverbs of Solomon son of David, king of Israel:[48]
2 for gaining wisdom and instruction;
for understanding words of insight;
3 for receiving instruction in prudent behavior,
for doing what is right and just and fair;
4 for giving prudence to those who are simple,
knowledge and discretion to the young ---
5 let the wise listen and add to their learning,
and let the discerning get guidance ---
6 for understanding proverbs and parables,
the sayings and riddles of the wise.
7 The fear of the Lord is the beginning of knowledge,
but fools despise wisdom and instruction.
8 Listen, my son, to your father's instruction
and do not forsake your mother's teaching.
9 They are garland to grace your head
and a chain to adorn your neck.
10 My son, if sinful men entice you,
do not give in to them.
11 If they say, "Come along with us
let's lie in wait for innocent Blood,
let's ambush some harmless soul;
12 let's swallow them alive, like the grave,
and whole, like those who go down to the pit;
13 we will get all sorts of valuable things
and fill our houses with plunder;
14 cast lots with us;
we will all share the loot: ---
15 my son, do not go along with them,
do not set foot on their paths;..."

---

48 Proverbs 1-15

The 4th Week of Lent

Day 32, Saturday – Seek Jesus

"Jesus saith unto him, I am the way, the truth, and the life: no man cometh unto the Father, but by me."[49]

My Lord, I could not imagine the depths of Your unhappiness from the displeasure that we cause You daily. We ought to seek Your gift of love earnestly. We ought to fervently seek Your presence in our short moment of time here on earth, but we are hindered by our minds and bodies denying our innerself of Your grace. Our imperfect hearts humbly long for You and our eager souls wish to please You but the enemy who lingers in our weak thoughts places little devotion and small aspiration in us that we often end our days selfishly serving others forsaking what we intended to do for You.

Help us to be worthy to deliver ourselves wholeheartedly to You. Grant the lukewarm hearts neither to seek those things of pleasure nor be misdirected by the enemy in all things. May You let Your love be revealed in all hearts for only You O Lord could help us in this inner battle of ours. Bless us with Your grace in order for us to turn our lives of hopeful devotion with a burning love for You with all our affection, with vehement desire and complete reverence to You O Lord Jesus Christ, in whose name "every knee will bow down to and every tongue will acknowledge God."[50] Amen.

He seeks us, each one of us. He loves us individually, not as a whole.
May we be united to seek Him and love Him as a whole.

---

49 John 14:6
50 Romans 14:11

Meditation

*God, help this poor soul
to be able to reach out to You.
Make my heart to feel
Your everlasting love
for my interior to be pure and free
and be drawn to Your most
ever sweet holy heart.*

*By Your grace Lord,
help me that I may stand strong,
not poor nor weak
for how I desire to shout out Your name,
proclaim Your glory, serve You
and fall on my knees to worship,
sing, and praise You
for the rest of my living days.*

The 5th Week of Lent

Day 33, Fifth Sunday – Prayer for All to be Pardoned

*"First of all, then, I urge that supplications, prayers,
intercessions, and thanksgivings be made for all people, for
kings and all who are in high positions, that we may lead a
peaceful and quiet life, godly and dignified in every way.
This is good, and it is pleasing in the sight of God our
Savior, who desires all people to be saved and to
come to the knowledge of the truth."*[51]

Heavenly Father, how much greater would Your eternal
glory be if all are pardoned? With the help of all Your
saints, grant holy, religious and faithful people to pray, peti-
tion and intercede for all the innocent, the living as well as
the dead to know Your truth and be able to return Your
infinite love with their endless praise. What would it mean
to our souls if any one of our loved ones be lost in total
darkness, or end in the company of the enemy for all
eternity? We do not wish any harm to come to anyone,
pardon us all.

God of love, You created us in Your image out of love, let
love clothe us all, blanket us with Your everlasting love of
mercy, forgive us. You gave up Your divine human life in
the most atrocious torture, a love beyond measure, yet with
one simple lowly act of repentance from us, or a humble

---

[51] 1 Timothy 2:1-4

utter of repentance from our lips, and we're in Your loving heart. Blessed Savior, with Your unbelievable love and eternal forgiveness, dispel darkness in our world, in its stead let the sun cover us with Your flaming fire of light and love. Let Your eternal love bring all Your children to Your eternal kingdom, in Your holy name with the Holy Spirit whose glory is forever and ever I pray. Amen.

Involving God in everything we do will
lead us to a peaceful life.

Meditation

*O Guest
of my wretched soul,
despite my imperfection,
You desire even so to awaken
my poor spirit
to be altered as a new babe
to become a child of Your Kingdom.*

*Awake
O sleepy soul,
dare not to be defeated,
let the hand of God touch
your slow-spirited heart, and
let the path of your sole walk towards Him
without ever glancing back.*

*Loving Father,
whose creative inspiration
led all people to be born,
grant our soul to be enlightened
from all blindness of this world,
forgive the innocent and
sanctify the redeemed.*

The 5th Week of Lent

Day 34, Monday – Pray to be Born Again

"Jesus answered and said to him,
"Truly, truly I say to you, unless one is born again
he cannot see the kingdom of God."[52]

Eternal God, from generation to generation, people don't know who or what to believe in. With the verse above, and Your Son's quote saying that: "Except ye repent ye shall all likewise perish."[53] I pray for all to take to heart these verses making note of the word 'perish' for if every living soul would take what Jesus said seriously, every one would try to seek religion, look up Christianity, and most of all seek You my God. Rather than looking for Your truth, some turn away from it. There are disobedience, hatred, fear, sorrow and death shadowing over us. Our world is in chaos, there is war all over the world, unbelievers are growing in number, bombs are being built even in the poorest of nations threatening our whole world. Lord God, the ungodly are persecuting Your children, save us O Savior of our world. Come and save us all.

Almighty Father, transform us, grant us all to be 'Born Again' children that we may have a true faithful relationship with You. Grant us to be like a 'babe in Christ'. Bring us new food and drink that we may all receive Your Word and bear new seeds. Feed us all, nourish us, change our weeping

---

52 John 3:3
53 Luke 13:3,5

to rejoicing. Let there be a cry of joy at the sound of Your name, let there be peace here on earth as it is in heaven. Father, let there be peace I pray, let Your love flow from Your heart to ours together with Your Son and the Holy Spirit who lives forever and ever, I pray. Amen.

The way to the Lord is to talk and
turn to Him anytime, anywhere.

Meditation

The sufferings You endured,
how could hearts be so hardened?
Your work of mercy,
why do souls become tepid?
Why do the lukewarm hearts
not feel Your love?
When will they feel, or see,
when will they know?

You paid our sins with Your life.
With our sins, we would all perish
but through You we have a way.
Believe in You will send us to heaven,
but what of some good people
the innocent and stubborn ones?
Lord, bless not a soul to miss heaven.

By Your mercy and grace
grant us to escape the pain
and agony of eternal punishment.
Bless all your people to be transformed,
pierce our hearts with the fire of Your love
as you did to Your St. Paul who did serve You
and loved You on to his end.

The 5th Week of Lent

Day 35, Tuesday – Bless Virgin Mary

*"Blessed are you among women,
and blessed is the fruit of your womb!"*[54]

Blessed be the name of Mary, virgin and mother, who has received great gifts from God, who conceived in her womb the Son of God. The daughter most holy and ever full of grace, a supernatural mother whose radiance shines from heaven down to earth who lives to make intercessions for humankind.

Blessed be the great mother of God, Mary most holy, Empress and Lady in God's everlasting kingdom. Our true mother in heaven and on earth, pray for us whose souls are in need of your advocate and protection. On earth, I invoke your sweet name and my lips sing to you Ave, Ave, Ave Maria! Kindly bless my soul and those of my loved ones. Pray for us so we may live each moment of our lives in love and peace.

Praise be to God, the Sovereign Lord who exalted you eternally. Praise be to the Holy Trinity forever. Amen.

*May all hearts be illumined of God's gifts to His daughter,
the mother of His Son, and the spouse of the Holy Spirit.*

---

54 Luke 1:42

Meditation

Beautiful, beloved and blessed Virgin Mary,
mother of God, queen of heaven.
I praise you for your faithfulness to Your Son Jesus,
I honor you for your compassion to His sufferings, and
I exalt you for your devotion to draw sinners on to Him.
Through your intercessions, multitude of souls
escape darkness to a life of eternal light.

O virgin of virgins, purest of the pure,
blessed are you for your loving ways
for the Lord is with you.
I bless you O holy mother of God
who nourished baby Jesus from His youth.
I bless you O holy Virgin Mary
for all your immaculate divine assistance.
I thank you my mother in heaven,
for your everlasting love and mercy.

The 5th Week of Lent

Day 36, Wednesday – Pray for the Breath of God

"He breathed on them, and saith unto them,
Receive ye the Holy Ghost."[55]

O Transcendent and Almighty God, as I sit quietly before the glory of Your heaven, I am in awe of all the wonders of You. You fill the night with stillness and silence as stars shine bright, Your peace and love surround this glorious night. O Eternal God of heaven You who breathed Your Spirit into the lives of devoted men and women; who formed minds with thoughts of You; who made their hearts to love You; and inclined their souls to hunger and thirst for You, breathe upon the door of my inmost being, in the same manner you breathed into all Your saints for my soul to be filled with Your fire divine, until my heart is made true, just and pure.

O Everlasting Breath of God, who made me for Yourself and breathed upon the first man created, lead me to a life of praising and magnifying Your name that I may one day see the glory of Your heaven and all the wonder of You. Let not my soul be restless until I repose in Your everlasting arms. Amen.

Some quiet times with the Lord makes the soul content.

---

55 John 20:22

Meditation

O good Holy Spirit of God, divine light
let our prayers come before You,
incline your ear to our voice.
Come and breathe Your Spirit of life into us,
richly nourish our heart and soul with
your refreshing glory.

Bestow blessings upon our poor heart
that we may be engulfed with desire
for Your truth and salvation.
O pure Spirit, convert our souls
that we may love as You love,
for us to be worthy to bless You at all times.

Bless our lips to praise You,
our souls to sing You songs,
and our mouths to magnify Your name
for as long as there is life in us.
All for the glory and magnificence of You,
the light of heaven and earth
who is all-pure, bright and brilliant
of all things in heaven and on earth.

The 5th Week of Lent

Day 37, Thursday – Blessed Assurance

*"And this is the testimony: God has given us eternal life,
and this life is in his Son. Whoever has the Son has life;
whoever does not have the Son of God does not have life.* [56]

O Lord Almighty, Creator of the whole world and its preserver, You desire for all men to be saved and to come to the knowledge of the truth, for there is one God, and one mediator between You and men, the man Christ Jesus.[57] Make us all realize what Your disciple St. John said in the above verse and to know that You have provided the way to our salvation through Your Son Jesus Christ. Bless us with Your promise of eternal life with You in Your heavenly kingdom by granting us all to believe in Your Son that we may be saved, including our household and by solemnly confessing with our heart and soul that He is our Lord and Savior who came down from heaven, who lived with us, died, was resurrected, and now lives with You in Your heavenly kingdom.

Lord God, grant our minds to be aware of Your light and the enemy's darkness after this life. Bless our mouths to proclaim our faith as Christians, and bless all hearts to love

56 John 5:11-13
57 1 Timothy 2:5

and believe in Your Son Jesus Christ, as it is written in Scriptures, "it is with the heart that we believe and are justified, and it is with our mouth that we profess faith and are saved."[58]

Let us make new memories of the present
and the future with God in it.

---

58 Romans 10:10

Meditation

How I rejoice the thought of You my friend,
You who dwell in my heart,
who when I was an innocent child
came forth Your presence by my side
and when fears overpower me,
who but You came to comfort me.

How I rejoice the thought of You my friend,
You who dwell in my heart,
who lovingly attend to my cries.
You who guard my ways and never give up,
who when my soul was insecure,
who but You came to comfort me.

Allow me to come to You my friend
and let me dwell in Your heart
that I may offer You my whole self
You who always make my heart at peace.
Let me come to comfort You my friend
with my undying love.

The 5th Week of Lent

Day 38, Friday – Give Up Spirit

"Enter his gates with thanksgiving, and his courts with praise! Give thanks to him; bless his name!"[59]

We thank You O God for the glory of all the days and nights we receive from You. May our prime thoughts as we open our eyes and close our eyes to sleep be on You daily. As we enjoy life's pleasures through Your tender mercy, and as we savor the wonderment of Your creation, guide us throughout this life's journey to walk closer to You each day of our lives and may we be blessed to behold Your glorious countenance and delight in Your love as we hopefully enter Your pure and loving heart when we give up our spirits on our last day.

O Savior of all things, of the living and the dead, pardon our offences I humbly beg for when our souls should depart from our bodies, we know that we will have to face You and be judged at that appointed time. As we are all sinners and guilty of your Holy Commandments, pardon us at the hour of our death, blot out our sinfulness. Even though we are not fit for heaven, protect our souls from evil powers to be protected by Your heavenly angels to safely carry us to Your heavenly kingdom to live and be with You forever. Blessed and praised be to You O Savior of the world, Jesus Christ who saved us by Your precious Blood. Amen.

*In the beginning was the Word that if we follow
will take us to the Lord in the end, for He is the Word.*

---

59 Psalm 100:4

Meditation

O heavenly God, almighty and merciful Lord,
for love, You died on the Cross, and
into the Father's hands You gave up Your Spirit.
You in whose hands are life and death
who casts down and raises us up,
have mercy on our souls,
raise us up on our last day.
Grant us the assistance of the Holy Spirit,
the blessings of a merciful death for
we know not when we will be called.

When our time to leave this world is near,
grace us to remember O loving Savior
of the Blood You shed,
Your agony on the Cross
and Your death for our salvation
to be our refuge and consolation.
Into Your hands O most merciful Lord,
receive our souls to be redeemed
not to die nor be lost, but to live
and be with You in Your heavenly kingdom
at last forever and ever.

The 5th Week of Lent

Day 39, Saturday – Draw Us To You

"No man shall be able to stand before you all the days of your life. Just as I was with Moses, so I will be with you. I will not leave you or forsake you. Be strong and courageous, for you shall cause this people to inherit the land that I swore to their fathers to give them."[60]

Beloved Jesus, on to Your Father out of this world, You gave up Your Spirit, You passed away to be in Your heavenly kingdom. You lived and led a life full of hardships and sufferings to Your death, yet You forgave everyone including Your executioners who were in darkness. We ought to know the real You, we ought to be sad and grieved by Your sufferings and death, we ought to remember those spikes when they nailed You to Your Cross, and we ought to cry out for Your forgiveness. Like Your executioners who lived in darkness, bless us to leave the dark room of our interior to let Your light shine in.

Bless us to follow Your lead for we have not the power You have especially when fears overpower us. We cannot do anything without hope and faith in You. Let us not fail and fall but instead lift us up that You may draw us to Yourself in order for us to be in the light with You and be able to open up our hearts to You. Let not darkness ensue us, I pray.

---

60 Joshua 1:5-6

Come O Lord, draw us on to You. Come through the locked doors of our hearts, open them to let us breathe out peace. Let us experience Your unconditional love by coming in through the inner soul of our hearts and souls that we may be touched by You, O Lord, united along with the Father and the Holy Spirit who reigns forever. Amen.

May God draw us up to Him to be among the presence of the blessed in the days to come.

Meditation

In God's body
You took upon Yourself to be the servant
though You have everything.
You humbled Yourself to be the lowest
to the point that You broke and bled.

In God's body
You took our punishment,
You spoke in silence
through Your trials and tribulations
to the point that You suffered and died.

In God's body
You could have been invincible, but did nothing
yet we, who are nothing and could do nothing
persecuted You, to death.
Forgive us Lord, please forgive us.

The 6th Week of Lent

Day 40, Palm Sunday – Passion of the Lord

"Rejoice greatly, O daughter of Zion; shout, O daughter of Jerusalem: behold, thy King cometh unto thee: he [is] just, and having salvation; lowly, and riding upon an ass, and upon a colt the foal of an ass." [61]

Lord Jesus, the Messiah, the Son of God, who would conquer the world, a righteous King who will execute justice and judgment upon the earth did not come with a mighty horse but rather rode upon an ass, as an example of humility. Beloved Jesus, You knew that You were to the point of Your own death when You entered Jerusalem amidst the cheering multitude, but through Your precious Blood, we prisoners of our own sins, have hope, for if we believe and turn to You with faith, through our trials and tribulations we will be saved. Thank You Jesus for Your encompassing love, a Love so patient that even when we ignore You, You persist to show us Your love. Even when we offend You, You continue to forgive us. You are so forgiving that You suffered willingly for us. You even picked up the heavy Cross to die for us. Our sins are too great that You could hardly carry Your Cross. You fell three times, yet none of us were there to help, none of Your friends not even Your disciples that the guard had to get Simon from Cyrene to help You on Your way to Calvary as You laid down Your life for our sins.

---

61 Zechariah 9:9

Merciful Lord, You showed us Your undying love, how should we return the love You have shown us? We're only but dusts of the earth who will all one day turn to ashes. We are Your humble servants yet You had freed our souls, that we pray, may one day be free to live forever, not just forever, but with You, in heaven! Bless us that we may praise You forever. Let us rejoice in You O Lord, that we may call upon Your name as our Savior forever and always. Praise to You our Lord Jesus Christ, King of endless glory! Alleluia to our Paschal Lamb. Amen.

Jesus is the Son of God, for God refers to Him as "my son".

Meditation

O divine Lord Jesus, our true life,
in whom, by whom and through whom,
all things live. Blessed are You who have
traveled from heaven over a tempestuous
life down to earth and into the narrow
alleys of Jerusalem where You were
triumphantly cheered.

Hail to the King, they shouted on the streets
where You knew what lies ahead,
You knew that You were to be the lamb
from Calvary's road down to the Cross.
You humbled Yourself until death
that You may save sinners and bring
life back into our world.

Jesus, Lamb of God, help us to know
the infallible truth of Your life, death
and resurrection. May all come to know
and be in awe of Your life's eternal
offering so we, with one voice, one heart
and one soul may sing to You with our unending
joy, praising Your glory for You are our
King, O holy, holy Lord.

The 6th Week of Lent

Day 41, Monday of Holy Week – Pray for the Sick and the Poor

"You shall serve the LORD your God, and he will bless your bread and your water, and I will take sickness away from among you."[62]

Our great Physician, gentle Healer of the sick, forgive us for our selfishness at times when we neglect to show our compassion to the sick and the poor. May we be unselfish at all times and go the extra mile to help the needy. Bless our eyes Lord to see those people not only in our own backyard but also those people throughout the world who live and die of sickness and hunger, everyday.

Our Comforter and Strength of sufferers, may we all acknowledge to place our worries, pain and sufferings into Your Hands. May we also learn to place our trust in You that whatever Your Will for us, is for a holy purpose. Merciful Lord, bless all hearts especially the ones with abundant resources to share their wealth and gifts, to show concern and sympathy to the helpless and the hopeless. May the prayers of those who cry out to You be heard, and may they rejoice to learn that Your mercy is upon them during their affliction. Lord God, make us all be worthy to serve everyone in need. In Your most beautiful and blessed name, holy Jesus with the Holy Spirit, we pray. Amen.

We can overcome challenges if we trust in His care.

---

62 Exodus 23:25

97

Meditation

Lord God,
You are merciful
good and gentle blessing us
with Your constant love and care.
As we delight in our youth,
living strong and actively
serving only our selfish pride,
grant Lord that we may not fail
to serve You rather than our
own worldly ambition.

Lord God,
when we're old
and sick, let our affliction
be our means to reach out to You,
to know Your presence by our side,
to feel Your sweetness in our hearts.
Let this be a time for us to think of You,
to worship You and be aware that
we can do nothing because we are
nothing, without You.

The 6th Week of Lent

Day 42, Tuesday of Holy Week – Pray for Deliverance

*"Listen to me, you islands; hear this, you distant nations:
Before I was born the Lord called me; from my mother's
womb he has spoken my name. He made my mouth like a
sharpened sword, in the shadow of his hand he hid me; he
made me into a polished arrow and concealed me in his
quiver. He said to me, "You are my servant, Israel,
in whom I will display my splendor." "*[63]

Lord God, we who love You and believe in You remain still
and pray to be blest to live this life worthy of Your calling.
Herein we hold our cups and calmly await for them to be
filled that we may see the firstfruits of the Spirit. We pray
for our deliverance from the bondage of our body's corrup-
tion as our souls hope for that glorious day of liberty. May
we receive the redemption of our bodies saved by hope. We
trust in Your sovereignty O God to soon come.

Father, Your Son fasted 40 days with no food, drink nor
sleep and did so to praise You. Grant us with the same
strength, determination, power and pure hearts that we may
glorify You in heaven with unending hymn of praise. May
Your kingdom come, Your Will be done on earth as it is in
heaven, in the blessed and holy name of our Savior Jesus
Christ, I pray. Amen.

*Jesus is forever with us. He is building a home for us
to stay with Him forever.*

---

63 Isaiah 49:1

Meditation

Holy Lord, You know our daily toil,
our hard labor on the long narrow road,
as You stated: "I know your deeds,
your hard work and your perseverance."[64]
You know the strength we've spent,
the weariness we bore,
we're thirsty, hungry and alone
with cups unfilled and empty plates.

But we know You'll fill our empty vessels,
we who walk the rugged roads and hills
will be filled with divine refreshment.
Though we must wait, we will hold our cups
until You come Beloved Jesus
for You, who asks us to be still
will await the coming of Your kingdom
here on earth as it is in heaven.

---

64 Rev. 2:2

The 6th Week of Lent

Day 43, Wednesday of Holy Week – Stay with Jesus

"And I will pour out a spirit of compassion and
supplication on the house of David and the inhabitants
of Jerusalem, so that, when they look on the one
whom they have pierced, they shall mourn for him,
as one mourns for an only child, and weep bitterly over him,
as one weeps over a firstborn. "[65]

Blessed Lord Jesus, as I journey with You this week, help me to stay with You during Your suffering. Let me not look the other way but rather give me the strength to watch and learn from Your love. With Your great need to meet us, You went up to Jerusalem to enter into Your glory through pain and suffering. Out of Your yearning for our love, You allowed us to crucify You and pierce You by Your side to be lifted up to heaven through your death on the Cross. On that very cross you forgave us our sins before you breathed your last breath, and by Your death and resurrection You redeemed us. Your Cross is now our tree of life that gives us fruit and hope to eternal life. Thank You Jesus for the life You gave.

With Your unwavering love beyond all others, You poured out Your Spirit of life for us, help us to understand Your passion and death, help us to have the endurance to stay

---

65 Zechariah 12:10

with You and mourn sorrowfully at Your feet to ask for Your forgiveness. Lord Jesus, bless us to amend ourselves by learning to bear our own cross renouncing our own selfish desires and pray for Your will to be done not ours. Amen.

Jesus let out a loud cry to His Father.
Let us cry out His name with love.

Meditation

*In the Upper Room
the disciples communed
where the Son of man came
not to be served but to serve, and
to give His life as ransom for many.*

*Judas Iscariot, the betrayer
who for love of money
was indwelt by sin asked:
"Surely it is not I? Lord"
for he himself was deceived
by the serpent himself.*

*Woe to the traitor, by whom
the Son of man was betrayed
for thirty pieces of silver.
It would be better for him
if he had never been born
for great was his sin.*

*Lord, from the inner room
of our souls, please forgive us,
for surely we have sinned against You.
Grant us to offer our lives
by serving You.*

The 6th Week of Lent

Day 44, Holy Thursday – The Lord's Supper

*"Be devoted to one another in love.
Honor one another above yourselves."*[66]

We become closer to You through our fervent prayers, and we tend to come closer to our brothers and sisters and all those around us through Your presence within us. Lord, there are times when we do not hear Your voice within or we do not recognize Your presence inside our souls, please forgive us for failing to acknowledge You. Forgive us for not fully showing our love to our friends or neighbors. Forgive us for our failure to love one another as You have commanded us to, for when we fail, we disappoint You and disobey Your commandment. Help us to learn to put others' interests ahead of our own, for as we learn to be humble, meek, kind, forgiving and patient among others, we become pleasing to You and united with You through love.

We get united through love, as most man and woman who are married. It's been written how marriage should be held sacred. May we honor all marriage between a man and a woman, undefiled, for You will judge the adulterer and all the sexually immoral. May all married men and women love each other perfectly; and may they love their children perfectly as well for they are not the fruit of man's labor,

---

66 Romans 12:10

"they are a gift from the Lord, a reward from You."[67] Help us all to become one united family. "Teach us O Lord to love one another as You have loved us. By this everyone will know that we are Your disciples, if we love one another as You have commanded us to."[68] By Your undying love Lord Jesus, who lives and reigns with the Father and the Holy Spirit, I pray. Amen.

May we all realize what Jesus had done for us.

---

67 Psalm 127:3
68 John 13:34-35

Meditation

As we journey on this life,
we notice God's beautiful gifts
that bring joy to every soul.
We delight ourselves with
life's richness that often
we fall short to notice others' tears,
troubles, pain and sufferings.

Lord, whose love You put
into the hearts of humans,
let us pilgrims of this world
show that love for one another that
with just a little show of kindness
a simple hello, a soft touch of the hand,
a heartfelt wish, a quick visit to the sick,
a gentle greeting, or a short prayer,
could help take away one's grief.
Grant us to be devoted to one another
in love.

The 6th Week of Lent

Day 45, Good Friday – Passion of the Lord

*"And I will pour on the house of David and on the
inhabitants of Jerusalem the Spirit of grace and
supplication; then they will look on me
whom they pierced...."*[69]

Lord of Power and Might, I will follow You whose way is
perfect. I will walk with You in faith and cast all my care to
You for You are my Judge. You died upon the Cross, let me
also bear my cross loving You til my end for You are my
hope and my refuge. I cherish You and Your Cross for it is
my salvation, my joy, my strength and my life eternal.

Your Cross is the height of all and is the meaning of life and
death. Lord, our affliction, grief, pain in mind or body, or
our soul's tribulations are nothing compared to what You
had gone through. I don't long for this life's comfort, ease of
mind, honor or reward from anybody, all I want is to follow
You as Your Saints did, and were able to, by Your grace,
lived all the way to their end, who also rose from their death
and entered Your heavenly glory. O what great profit to reap
an everlasting reward for surrendering ourselves to You
Lord. By Your grace prepare me, and grant me the strength
to make my flesh bear whatever You will for me that I may

---

69 Zechariah 12:10

have life through You Jesus Christ, our Lord, through whom all glory is given forever and ever with the Father and the Holy Spirit. Amen.

Daily life lived in silence, faith and hope
are daily peace with God.

Meditation

O holy, holy, holy Lord!
Whose unthinkable passion
drove You to enter our world.
Was there no other way to save us?

Born from a virgin
with a perfect heart and a spotless soul,
Your earthly life has just begun.
O young Son of God,
why did it have to be You?

Despising shame,
You agonized for us
to where love led You to the tree.
O Jesus, how could I ever repay You
except for my poor and humble heart.

At the Stations of the Cross

Introduction

Love, there are no words to express Jesus' unconditional love; His love for the Father, and His love for His lovely mother Virgin Mary who loved Him so deeply from the beginning to His end. O blessed Mother, there are no words to the pain and sorrow you felt when you saw Your beloved Son went through all His suffering. It must have been unbearable to hear the crowd's cheer of hate towards Him and to see His bloody face and body as He carried the Cross while being beaten and tortured. Where did you get the strength to watch Him stumble and fall with no friends around to help Him? And most of all, when they took His lifeless body down from the Cross and You held Him one last time, how did you do it?

You felt His pain and sorrow but You too were silent just as He was. He never spoke a word though He was innocent. Even up to now, we are still persecuting Him, doubting and questioning who He is. Pray for us O holy mother, pray for us to understand why He died on the Cross that we may feel a pierce in our hearts for sorrow, shame and repentance to enter into our souls.

Opening Prayer

In the name of the Father, and of the Son, and of the Holy Spirit. Amen. Father, in the Old Testament, through Your prophets You introduced us to the birth of Your Son, Jesus Christ, and through Your prophet Isaiah (53:3-9 below), You foretold of His sufferings and death. Step by step, very clear and concise were Isaiah's prophecies. Father, grant us to discern and acknowledge Your Son's humble and most sorrowful life, His sufferings and crucifixion on the Cross, His sacrificial death and His resurrection to His glory.

Isaiah 53:3-9
"3 He was despised and rejected by mankind, a man of suffering, and acquainted with infirmity; and as one from whom others hide their faces, he was despised, and we held him of no account. 4 Surely he has borne our infirmities and carried our diseases; yet we accounted him stricken, struck down by God, and afflicted. 5 But he was wounded for our transgressions, crushed for our iniquities; upon him was the punishment that made us whole, and by his bruises we are healed. 6 All we like sheep have gone astray; we have all turned to our own way, and the Lord has laid on him the iniquity of us all. 7 He was oppressed, and he was afflicted, yet he did not open his mouth; like a lamb that is led to the slaughter, and like a sheep that before its shearers is silent, so he did not open his mouth. 8 By a perversion of justice he was taken away. Who could have imagined his future? For he was cut off from the land of the living, stricken for the transgression of my people. 9 They made his grave with the wicked and his tomb with the rich, although he had done no violence, and there was no deceit in his mouth."

O beloved Jesus, thank You for the precious life You gave. Lord, forgive us, help us to understand the price You paid so that we may place ourselves on each step of the Way of Your Cross.

Act of Contrition. O my God, I am heartily sorry for having offended Thee, and I detest all my sins because of Thy just punishments, but most of all because they offend Thee, my God, who art all-good and deserving of all my love. I firmly resolve, with the help of Thy grace, to sin no more and to avoid the near occasions of sin.

Prayers on the Way of the Cross

Jesus Christ humbly carried the Cross and sacrificed His Deity in order for us to have salvation. In honor of our Lord's final hours of His life on earth to open heaven for us, let us pray.

Station 1. You were condemned to death. You were innocent but You accepted death for our sake. O God, help us to have faithful hearts til our end. I will adore You and praise You forever.

Station 2. You bent over, You were made to bear the heavy cross. Lord, I wish to come after You. Help me to embrace my cross, feel and bear its weight in silence.

Station 3. You stumbled, You fell the first time. The weight of the Cross is too much but You have a divine destiny. Lord, help me not to stumble and fall. Lead me to find my way to You.

Station 4. Your mother, You met Your afflicted mother. The blessed Virgin pained when she saw You but in difficulty she stood by You. Lord, allow me to comfort You. Bless me with hands and feet to serve You the rest of my life.

Station 5. You were near collapse, Simon was seized to help You carry Your Cross. Lord, bless me with a faithful heart ready to help anyone in need. Bless me to take up my daily cross.

Station 6. Your bleeding face, Veronica wiped Your face. God, grant me a heart filled with love for my neighbors in need that I may stop and help.

Station 7. You were exhausted, You fell the second time. Oh Jesus, how great Your suffering was due to my sins. Jesus, keep me from temptations and give me strength to walk with You.

Station 8. You were touched by their tears, You spoke to the daughters of Jerusalem to ask them to pray for their children, for the dreadful destruction was to come to Jerusalem. As I embrace You wholeheartedly my Lord, lift up my sorrows and answer my prayers for I trust in You.

Station 9. You were in agony, You fell the third time. Oh my Lord, I would pick up Your Cross if I were there and carry it for You. Touch my spirit to be willing to bear other's burdens to make my heart in accord with Yours.

Station 10. You were stripped of everything, You were stripped of Your garments. My heart melts as they stripped You naked. Clothe me with righteousness, help me to give what I possess that is of value to the poor, and give over my body to hardship.

Station 11. You were crucified, You were nailed to the Cross. They have pierced Your hands and feet. My heart felt pierced. Lord, if I were there, I would take Your place so You could rest awhile as I hang on Your Cross. I will call Your name.

Station 12. You died on the Cross, it is finished. You died loving us and conquered the world. Lord, may we all have courage to share in Your pain. Bless us to have peace. I give my life to You.

Station 13. Your body hangs on the Cross, You were taken down from Your Cross. Our mother Virgin Mary held You one last time. My soul is anguished, my heart grieves as I mourn for You, my Beloved, do not leave, be in my humble heart always.

Station 14. You were lifeless, You were placed in the sepulcher. Lord, help me know the worthlessness of my human body. Grant me to rid myself of vanity and reach out only for the beauty of heavenly things. Lord, I love you, I venerate Your Cross and I praise Your Resurrection. Amen.

In the words of our Savior, let us pray:

Our Father, who art in heaven, hallowed be thy name; Thy kingdom come, Thy will be done on earth as it is in heaven. Give us this day our daily bread, and forgive us our trespasses, as we forgive those who trespass against us; and lead us not into temptation, but deliver us from evil. Amen.

To the Almighty Father

I believe that You are a Spirit God. I believe in the Holy Spirit who lives inside of me. I believe that You could hear my every whisper. I believe that You could feel my heart and You could see deep inside my soul. I believe in Your holy church, in the blessed Virgin Mary, mother of God, in the holy Body and the precious Blood of Your Son Jesus Christ in the Sacrament; and I believe in all Your mysteries including the sanctification, purification and glorification of all Your Saints.

I believe in Your Son Jesus Christ, our Lord and Savior, who came, lived, suffered and was crucified for my sins so I may live with You, with Him and the Holy Spirit for all eternity. I believe that He will come again to give His judgment to the living and the dead, all of whom would rise that day and be judged; thereupon, love, peace and joy will be on earth forever. I believe in the Trinity with all of my mind, might, heart and soul. In the name of Jesus I pray. Amen.

The 6th Week of Lent

Day 46, Holy Saturday – Easter Vigil in the Holy Night of Easter

"When he had cried with a loud voice, he said,
Father, into your hands I commend my spirit –
and having said this, he gave up the spirit."[70]

O loving Jesus, at this time of year, I am reminded of Your painful death with Your hands stretched out upon the Cross, "and being in an agony you prayed more earnestly: and your sweat was as it were great drops of Blood falling down to the ground."[71] Nothing remained in You for You gave up Your entire holy Self to death, so that You could fulfill the prophecy and to appease the Father's disappointment, His anguish and pain that He may be reconciled with our unworthy souls.

You went through horrors in full submission for us to know the depths of Your love. For us to need and desire You, to sigh and sorrow upon Your excruciating pain and sufferings, You went through disgrace, filth and hatred, whips and blows with thorns of crown pressed upon Your scalp, and the torture You received from ungrateful humans before Your obscene crucifixion were all for your unequivocal thirst for us to perceive You.

70 Luke 23:46
71 St. Luke 22:44

From the Cross, You passed the doorway from death to life. Then out of this world You handed over Your Spirit, an immortal Spirit that belonged to the Father where it went back in Your heavenly kingdom. With Your triumphant cry: "It is finished!" You left our world, You breathed Your last breath, laid down Your precious Life of Your own free will, voluntarily, that no one, nothing, and no enemy can take away from You. And having said thus, You gave up the Holy Ghost.

We cannot change the past, but we can do
God's will to change our future.

Meditation

Crowned with piercing thorns,
wounded, reviled and scorned,
"You gave Your back to those who strike
and Your cheeks to those who pull out Your beard,
You hid not Your face from disgrace and spitting.[72]
Your appearance so marred beyond human semblance,
and Your form beyond that of the children of mankind.[73]
Bleeding and dying, You endured the Cross.

From this land of exile out of life's raging storm,
You exhaled your last breath; Your death, our salvation.
O Lord Jesus Christ, who hung upon for our sins,
a lump of clay though I be, I come to You
from my home of exile, out of this land of raging storm,
raise me, draw me to You for by Your Cross,
forever I would cling to, that I may rise with You
til I leave this life behind.

---

72 Isaiah 50:6
73 Isaiah 52:14

Easter Sunday – Resurrection of the Lord

"Jesus [said], "I am the resurrection and the life; whoever believes in me, even if he dies, will live, and everyone who lives and believes in me will never die."[74]

Almighty Father, thank You for Jesus. Thank You for Your Son's mystical journey with us here on earth who came with the spirit of truth and guidance to give us eternal salvation through His death and resurrection. Thank You for His passion and suffering that were witnessed by many including His apostles and disciples. "After his suffering, he presented himself to them and gave many convincing proofs that he was alive. He appeared to them over a period of forty days and spoke about the kingdom of God."[75] He ascended into the heaven right in front of His apostles and now sits at Your right hand, the most high, praise to You O God!

Praise to You Lord Jesus Christ, thank You for Your powerful rising that we who believe declare You as the Son of God. Thank You for sharing Your divine life with us when You came as a man here on earth. May the mysteries of Your love, life, death and resurrection give us new life, an eternal life with You in heaven. Every human being should bow at the sound of Your name and proclaim Your great glory, O divine Lord, our Savior Jesus Christ! Praise, blessing and glory, wisdom and thanksgiving, honor, power and might to God the Father, His Son and the Holy Spirit forever and ever! Amen.

May we live an everlasting life because the truth is our life hasn't even begun.

---

74 John 11:25-26
75 Acts 1:3

Meditation

How lovely is Your face O Lord,
Your resplendent soul, Your holiness.
No word can express Your grandeur,
nor Your glorious kingdom.
Now at the right hand of the Father,
You are at the throne of God.

Brilliant and dazzling are You
with radiance ever so sweet.
Your glory is of immense riches and delight,
great are You who sits on Your throne.
My lips will forever praise You my Lord
and my soul shall glory in You forever!

The Gospel of John 20:29

"Blessed are they that have not seen,
and yet have believed."[76]

You asked us to remain united with You,[77] Lord I trust and lean on You. You invite us to come to You and You will give us rest,[78] Lord, I will rest fully on You and busy myself for You because I truly believe in You. With the fire of Your love, may You ignite all souls to believe in You, and may You breathe on us to receive the Holy Spirit. Let the wind of Your Holy Spirit make us proclaim You as our one and only God, as did Your disciples, who saw You performed other miraculous signs besides the ones recorded so that all may believe that You are the Messiah, the Son of God, and that by believing in You, we will have eternal life.

In Your great mercy, You drew some unworthy souls such as this one to You who do not deserve anything. In my weakness, may I never in my life forget that day of blessing, the hour I first believed. May I never forget all the blessings You have bestowed upon me and my loved ones ever since. May I be reminded of Your sorrows, sacrifices, sufferings and finally death that I may always be blest to be near You in Spirit, through my faith and contrition. In repentance for my sins, I pray for the forgiveness of the faithless, the

---

76 John 20:29
77 John 15:4
78 Matthew 11:28

ungodly, and unbelievers. Lord, enlighten them to know You that they may escape the dark torture of death, but rather see the brightness of Your glorious heaven; and Lord, bless them to be among the blessed that have not seen, yet have believed! Amen.

Life here on earth ends, but a life with Jesus never ends.

Meditation

What is vision?
Is it simply a power of the eyes
in anticipation of what is to come?
or perhaps it's a credibly vivid
experience influenced by the divine.

By God's grace,
He makes our eyes to see the light
to perceive a vision to be transformed
into an image perceived through the mind
down to our heart and soul.

How blessed were the ones
whose eyes saw Jesus when He walked
among men. Those who ate with Him,
those present when He taught, healed and
prayed to His Father.

How blessed are the eyes
that have not seen Jesus' crucified,
who didn't see His body taken down
from the Cross, and were not there
to see nor touch His wounded side,
and yet have believed!

Meditations

In remembrance of our Lord's sacred visit in our world, let us continue to follow him and remind ourselves of His lone purpose which is solely for our sake. The mystery in the Upper Room will help remind us the evening during the last sacred meal.

Dark and mysterious was the night,
a betrayal was plotted on that painful night
that would never be forgotten
in the history of mankind.

God allowed sin upon this eve of forgiving.
Peter a disciple betrays the Lord three times,
while Judas who hates, waits without fear,
led Jesus to His Cross.

Judas preferred darkness to the light
for evil was within him, so he perished.
Anyone who lives by the truth
and believes sees the light.
Lord, grant us true faith to save our soul.

Jesus, grant us to change for the better, grant us all to hear and listen to Your voice for our world to change.

One day unexpected
We will cease, one by one
Back to dust and ashes we shall be
Just like our forefathers years gone by.

Where will we be?
Who will remember us?
Behold, there is hope for all of us
A gift free from God Himself bestowed.

For God is love
He shall restore the faithful
His Promise never to be forgotten
Praise the Lord our God, He will save us.

Believe
Have faith in the Lord
One by one he will remember us
Penned with love in His Book of Life.

Jesus is hungry for our love, may we return His hunger by repentance of our sins and consecrate ourselves to Him.

Love who loves,
I beseeched You in whatever I did,
wherever I was and whichever way I turned
I looked for You for I was thirsty
in need of Your grace.

In Your warm love,
You looked upon this mere dust
and graciously You showed me
my unworthy soul to perceive my sins
so that I may be cleansed.

Blessed are You sweet Jesus
who is hungry for my love.
Acknowledging my own nothingness
for I am but dust and ashes
now I'm all Yours and You are mine.

As we continue to walk with our Lord day by day, let us ask Him to open our eyes to the fullness of His love that we may wholly and unconditionally return His love.

Make me hear
Make me know Your voice
Teach me how to find You and
Show me how this heart of mine
Can show You a love beyond measure.

O blessed One
Who radiates love
I will venerate Your Name
I will meditate Your hour of passion
I will immerse myself entirely in Your mercy.

God remains the same, season after season till the end of
time.

Weather, seasons, climate,
they all change
but You remain the same,
Your power is endless
and heaven is eternal.

Through all the passing time
with life's storms and tribulations
on this time-wheel of ours
Your love remains the same,
unchanged, perpetual.

Over life's perplexing existence
we remain unchanged,
divided by Your endless love.
Bless all hearts to love You,
bless us to follow You
til the end of time.

Every day is a new day. Thank You God for the ways You manifest Your presence in our lives, including the bright shining sun.

How wonderful it is to wake up
in the morning to see the sun shining
as I draw back the curtains
to smell the scent of roses and honeysuckle
while birds sing and flowers bloom.
You fill my world with radiance
and make my heart rejoice.

How beautiful this world is
enlightened by Your light
as I welcome the soft breeze
upon my cheeks
coming from Your warm embrace.
Oh what precious gifts
these gentle touch from heaven above.

Once in a while, we need to clean up and trim down bushes and small branches that are obstructing our window's view. This way, we see more sunlight, flowers and evergreens and enjoy the beauty of the outside more; as if our eyes were closed before, but now we can see more clearly.

In my sleep You have awakened me
To my sins and weaknesses
With a sorrowful and repenting soul
For all the years I've wasted
I turned to You my Lord.

You caused me pain deep inside that
To be with You became my goal.
With anxious heart and eager soul
I lifted up my eyes to heaven
To try and find You.

Into my blindness You made me see
You came to save me from my sins
You cleansed me night after night
Now I long for You day after day
Since You've awakened me
From my deep, deep sleep.

Through our walk with Jesus, we have learned that He abandoned Himself for us willingly. He has given us Earth and now He is offering us Heaven. By accepting, we have nothing to lose but gain everlasting life and the love of God for eternity.

Why did.....
Your friend betrayed You?
You have to be beaten so harshly?
they crown You with thorns?
You have to carry a heavy Cross?
You have to fall three times?
they nail Your Hands and Feet?
You have to hung on the Cross?
You have to pay for our sins?
You have to die?

Was it to.....
show us how to be humble?
let us know how to love one another?
for us to know the Father?
fulfill the Scriptures?
teach us how to pray?
reveal who You are?
guide us to heaven?
transform us?
follow You?

Or was it.....
a cry for peace?
to be intimate with You?
simply because of love?
Yes, it's an act of love.
You died for all,
You did it all for love,
the mystery is solved!
Jesus, Savior of the World
Thank You, thank You God!

Lord, take my hand and lead me out of the shadow of darkness into the brightness of Your light.

In the midst of the sky last night I found myself flying
along the beach serene where my bare feet landed.
Though dark and desolate upon a seashore stars lit,
sparkling waters danced before my eyes.
The cold wind softly caressed my skin as
soft breeze whisked by my cheeks like a gentle kiss.
Each breath of the crisp cool air I took
was so delightful, I was enchanted.

While I savoured such sensations
suddenly a stranger appeared in sight
and greeted me with a gentle smile.
Shaken and surprised I thought
'who could this man be
and where did he come from?'
This man is no stranger in this place
the fact is often he came to visit said he.
"Do not be afraid" he exclaimed "for I mean no harm."
Peace then I felt upon his voice.

"Come, follow me" he commanded.
In the wink of an eye there we were transported
inside a cave wherein he showed me people.
The social group, they merrily pranced and danced
sung and cheered aloud in front a church.
Next, my eyes witnessed people,
they sat in pews inside a church
all calmed, collected and still
yet unmoved amidst the homily.

Things of nature he spoke thereafter.
Farther into the dark dismal dank of the abyss
he showed me more people walking
as if robots, minds blank, eyes blind
endlessly searching, lost
deep in this tunnel of darkness.
In silence, we continued to walk,
he paused on a rock where he sat,
then celestial speakings he taught me.

Out of the dark into the light we went,
our time was up.
I stared at his lovely face
from where I stood
I watched him in his white bright robe
as he walked away
through the thick fog
til He disappeared into the light.

At the end of all our daily routine, at the end of the day, and at the end of our life, everything boils down to one thing, that there is God. Jesus is real, and if we believe, we will live.

Lord,
in my poor estate
I, with no power seek You.
I, who not of my own will
became a being
will soon be turned to ashes
yet not of my own free will.
But through You
out of my own will
I will live,
my life will continue forever
with You, for I believe.

There is nothing in this world more satisfying than believing in Jesus Christ because He lets you know that He is near, that He cares, that He loves you and that there is nothing to worry about after this life because He'll be with You to the end.

O light of my life
You shine Your everlasting light
to the angels of the earth.
You give Your glorious heavenly gifts
to the apples of Your eyes,
and You send Your love and affection
to Your saintly doves.

Blessed are You who bring immense ocean
of sweetness to the souls who love You.
Your goodness brings holy love
to the children who bless You.
Grant Your tender mercy to all,
illumine Your beautiful Self to those
who walk in darkness, fill them
with Your Spirit of life.

Gently incline Your loving heart
to rest upon us all and let Your
boundless love be received by them
whose eyes have not seen You,
whose ears have not heard Your Word,
and whose hearts have yet to receive You
for all souls to worship and love You
till the end of time.

Closing Prayer

In the name of our Lord Jesus Christ, the Father, God of the Bible and God of peace. Amen. Father, we turn to You for You are our only source of true comfort and peace. Grant us to know the passion of Your Son Jesus Christ that we may live the life He tells us the way we should and that we may know the message He left to become evident in our world. Bless us with the knowledge to know the whole meaning of why He gave up His life; why He willingly died for us with His sacred Blood; let us know the reason and the purpose of His passion so that we may walk this life united in one belief that Your Son came to save sinners for love of You. Stricken by grief over Your sadness because of our sinfulness, He came down and became the Lamb to atone for our sins. It was not necessary nor was it a payment, it was a sacrificial act of love. [79]

Oh most glorious and magnificent Jesus, You could have come with all Your heavenly angels, with all the glory, bright and shining like a sparkling diamond, rather You came down from heaven enslaved by passion; from a babe to a young, poor man, from the poorest of the poor as like a piece of bread to be broken into pieces, for the Blood of slaughtered sheep were not enough to pay for our sins. You became the sacrificial lamb to atone for our sins. You opened not Your mouth, condemned though innocent, You bore our guilt and surrendered Yourself to death. You paid it all. Our whole life of praise and thanks are not enough for what You have done, we can only offer You our humble hearts filled with love for You. May we all look up to You

---

[79] Ephesians 5:2

in heaven, bow our heads as we ask for Your forgiveness and help.

We turn to You O God to help our weak souls and wicked world, grant our small minds not to put blame on You, or each other, nor condemn any race, creed, color, religion or origin. Grant all ears to hear that because of love, Your only-begotten Son died for our sins. He was pierced for our transgressions, he was crushed for our inequities; the punishment that brought us peace was on him, and by his wounds we are healed.[80] Thank You O Savior of the world, blessed Lord Jesus Christ for by Your life, death and resurrection, You have redeemed us.

Almighty God of heaven and earth, may all believe in Jesus Christ because it is of utmost importance as our salvation depends on it. [81] The Holy Bible made this fact loud and clear from the Old Testament to the New Testament. It also made clear that we humans have sinned[82] and the punishment for sin is death, but through Your Son we do not have to be separated from You for whoever believes in Him will have eternal life in heaven.

Eternal life in heaven forever and ever! It's an over-whelming, exhilarating, inspiring and unbelievable truth. May all minds grasp the truth about the suffering of Your Son Jesus in the hands of sinners, that with the help of wicked men, He was put to death by nailing Him to the cross.[83] Father, bless unbelieving hearts to accept His undying love who even while on His dying Cross said:

---

80 Isaiah 53:5
81 John 8:24
82 Romans 3:23
83 Acts 2:23

"Father, forgive them, for they do not know what they are doing."[84]

May Your Son's work of saving all of us be a time of the past; and may this generation and future generations be guided by Your Word; may all hearts and souls be touched and renewed from inside-out. Bless us the wisdom to know the truth, the strength to fight the enemy and the will to follow Jesus who is our bridge from earth to heaven. Praise and blessed be the name of Jesus Christ who had saved us by His precious Love, Holy Body and Sacred Blood, who lives and reigns with the Father and the Holy Spirit, one God forever and ever. Amen.

84 Luke 23:24

References

Holy Bible, New Revised Standard Version containing The Old and New Testaments, American Bible Society, New York. Copyright 1989.

The Holy Bible, containing the Old and New Testaments, Authorized (King James) Version, The National Bible Press, Philadelphia. Copyright 1963, The National Publishing Co.

The Holy Bible, New International Version, NIV, Copyright 1973, 1978, 1984, 2011 by Biblica.

The Holy Bible, New Living Translation, Copyright 1996, 2004, 2007. Used by permission of Tyndale House Publishers, Inc., Carol Stream, Illinois 60188.

The Holy Bible, English Standard Version. Copyright 2001 by Crossway Bibles, a publishing ministry of Good New Publishers.

Other Books by the Author:

Christ, My Passion, 2005

A Time for God, 2009

Prayers to Jesus, 2010

About the Author

Aida Rabenhorst's devotion to God and her recent pilgrimage brought her once again to write her fourth book, with the hope to spread the Word of God.

She invites you to use this book as a daily guide to pray and meditate.

In addition to her spiritual devotion, she enjoys spending part of her time with her two grandchildren. During her spare time, she does other creative outlet such as music (playing the piano), and art, including painting (mostly original religious ones).

CPSIA information can be obtained
at www.ICGtesting.com
Printed in the USA
LVHW110332140223
739353LV00007B/1443

9 781608 626366